World View: Iran's Struggle for Supremacy

Tehran's Obsession to Redraw the Map of the Middle East

John J. Xenakis

Xenakis Publishing — Generational Theory Book Series

Xenakis Publishing
Generational Theory Book Series

Digital ISBN: 978-1-7327386-0-7
Paperback ISBN: 978-1-7327386-1-4

Edition 1

Table of Contents

Part I. Introduction 8

    Chapter 1. Justification for this book 8

    Chapter 2. Fact-checking this book 11

Part II. Iran today and its internal conflicts 12

    Chapter 3. Student protests of 1999 12

    Chapter 4. More protests during the generational awakening of Iran's college students 15

    Chapter 5. The 2009 election and the Green movement 18

Part III. Iran in the 19th-20th centuries 20

    Chapter 6. Iran in the 1800s 21

    Chapter 7. History of Constitutions 25

    Chapter 8. Concessions, Capitulations and the Tobacco Revolt (1890-92) 28

        8.1. The Capitulatory System of the Middle East (1500s-1900s) 28

        8.2. The Tobacco Revolt (1890-92) 29

    Chapter 9. Iran's Constitutional Revolution (1905-09) 32

    Chapter 10. Iran after the Constitutional Revolution (1909-53) 34

        10.1. Iran during World War I 34

        10.2. Iran during World War II 35

        10.3. Anglo-Iranian Oil company nationalized, and 1953 CIA coup 35

    Chapter 11. The White Revolution (June 1963) and approach to 1979 revolution 39

        11.1. The White Revolution (June 1963) vs the Tobacco Revolt (1890) 39

        11.2. Prelude to the 1979 Great Islamic Revolution 41

Part IV. The Great Islamic Revolution (1979-present) 42

    Chapter 12. The rise of Ayatollah Ruhollah Khomeini 42

    Chapter 13. The 'causes' of the Great Islamic Revolution 44

    Chapter 14. The excuses for the Great Islamic Revolution 46

    Chapter 15. Khomeini's great massacre of 1988 49

    Chapter 16. Iranian hostage crisis 51

Part V. Pre-Islamic Persian empires...52
Chapter 17. The cycles of history.......................................52
Chapter 18. Summary of pre-Islamic Persian empires.............55
Chapter 19. Persian history — early dynasties.........................57
Chapter 20. Cyrus the Great and the Achaemenid Persian empire (550-331 BC)...60
Chapter 21. Alexander the Great and the Seleucid Empire (323-150 BC)...63
Chapter 22. The Arsacids and the Parthian Empire (247 BC-226 AD)..66
22.1. Arsaces I conquest of Parthia (247 BC) 66
22.2. Roman-Parthian Wars (53 BC - 217 AD)..................................... 66
Chapter 23. The Sassanid Empire (226-651 AD).....................68

Part VI. Persian history after the conquest by Islamic Arabs.....69
Chapter 24. The fall of the Sassanian Empire to the Islamic Arabs (630-651)..69
24.1. The war between the Sassanians and the Byzantines 69
24.2. The last Sassanian king, Yazdgird III.. 70
24.3. The Caliphs versus the Imams.. 71
24.4. The first Shia Imam: Ali Ibn Abi Talib (601-661) 72
24.5. The Hashim clan versus the Umayya clan 74
24.6. Ali becomes Caliph (656): Partisans of Ali = Shiat Ali = Shia 75
24.7. The Battle of Siffin (657) and the Kharijites and 'infidel' concept........... 77
24.8. Abdullah ibn Saba and the alleged Jewish origins of Shia Islam 77
24.9. Shia-Sunni clashes become vicious after Ali is assasinated (661)........... 79
Chapter 25. Battle of Karbala (October 10, 680) and beheading of al-Husayn...81
25.1. Prelude to the Battle of Karbala.. 81
25.2. The Battle of Karbala.. 81
25.3. Aftermath and the commemoration of Ashura 82
25.4. Hussaini Brahmans - the link between Shia Muslims and Hindus........ 82
Chapter 26. Expansion of the Islamic empire 84
26.1. Birth and death of empires — the cycles of history.................... 84
26.2. Zaydi Shia Muslims 85
26.3. The Battle of Zab (750) and the Abbasids................................. 85
26.4. The Banquet of Blood (750) 86
26.5. The Abbasid Dynasty (750-1258).. 86

Part VII. The Koran and Sharia (Islamic) law.....................87
Chapter 27. Development of Sharia law following Mohammed's death 87
Chapter 28. Roman Law versus Sharia (Islamic) law: The role of the Jurist 89

Chapter 29. There's no such thing as Sharia law 91
29.1. Misunderstandings about Sharia law 91
29.2. Mohammed's wives, and accusations of polygamy and pedophilia 92

Chapter 30. Disputes over the authenticity of the Bible 97

Chapter 31. Brief summary of the Koran 98
31.1. Money lending 98
31.2. Verses about marriage, divorce, dower, conjugal life, family disputes . 98
31.3. Koran verses about inheritance 99
31.4. The Koran on civil war among the faithful 99
31.5. Koran on business dealings and transactions 99
31.6. Koran on theft: cut off their hands 100
31.7. The Koran on fornication or obscene acts 100

Chapter 32. Disputes over the authenticity of the Koran 101

Chapter 33. Violence in the Koran: The sword-verses 104
33.1. The empirical evidence — Muslim nations governed by Sharia law ... 104
33.2. The empirical evidence — Muslim wars of invasion 105
33.3. The empirical evidence — Muslim populations involved in civil wars
.... 105
33.4. The empirical evidence — Extremist jihadists referencing Sharia law 106
33.5. The 'Sword-Verses' of the Koran and the Jizya 108
33.6. Comparison of the Koran's sword-verses to the Bible's Old Testament
.... 109
33.7. Comparisons of Jesus to Mohammed 110

Chapter 34. Disputes over the authenticity of the Sunnah and
Hadith 112

Chapter 35. There's no such thing as Sharia law - again 115

Chapter 36. Brief history of Catholic and Orthodox Christian
'Ecumenical' Councils 117
36.1. The Ecumenical Councils 117
36.2. The Seventh Ecumenical Council (787) - iconoclasts and iconophiles . 118
36.3. The Catholic vs Orthodox Christian schism (1054) 118
36.4. Universal versus regional religions 119

Chapter 37. Blasphemy and violence in Islam 121
37.1. Blasphemy laws in the UK and Ireland 121
37.2. The 2015 Paris Charlie Hebdo terrorist attacks 123
37.3. Iran's death fatwa against Salman Rushdie and 'Satanic Verses' 123

Part VIII. Shia Islam Theology 125

Chapter 38. The twelve infallible Imams 125
38.1. The Sunni-Shia theological split 125
38.2. Fivers, Seveners and Twelvers 126

Chapter 39. The disappearance of al-Mahdi and the rise of the
Shia jurists 127
39.1. The Occultation — the disappearance of the 12th Imam (940 AD) 127
39.2. The rise of Shia jurists and Shia jurisprudence 128
39.3. Sheikh Morteza Ansari and the Tobacco Revolt 128

39.4. Shia jurisprudence and the Constitutional Revolution.......................... 129

39.5. Theory of Wilayat al-Faqih (Guardianship of the Jurist)...................... 131

Part IX. Shia theology in practice under Khomeini 134

Chapter 40. Wilayat al-Faqih in practice 134

40.1. Divine guidance vs popular will 134

40.2. The third way: Corruption 135

40.3. The missing checks and balances 136

40.4. The Principlists versus the Reformists...................................... 138

Chapter 41. The Future of Iran 139

41.1. December 2017 protests - challenge to Supreme Leader's legitimacy.. 139

41.2. Replacing the Constitution.. 141

41.3. Selecting a successor to Supreme Leader Khamenei............................ 142

41.4. Regime change and generational awakening 143

Part X. The End 145

Chapter 42. About Generational Theory 145

Chapter 43. About John J. Xenakis 147

Chapter 44. Acknowledgments 149

Part XI. Footnotes / References...................................... 150

King Darius of the Persian Achaemenid empire offers a sacrifice to the Gods

Part I. Introduction

Chapter 1. Justification for this book

Ignorance of Islam in the West is cavernous. In my experience, this is even true among Muslims in the West. On top of that, what's going on in Iran is almost completely inscrutable in the West, even though Iran is in the news almost every day.

I know this because, as a journalist and analyst, I've written thousands of "World View" articles about Islam and Iran. I read comments posted to my articles. Most comments thank me for providing in-depth reporting not available in the mainstream media. But other commenters say that all Muslims should be deported and/or killed, and blame me for not saying so. These commenters are the most extreme of all, sometimes to the point of psychosis.

So based on thousands of articles on Islam and Iran that I've already written, the purpose of this book is to provide, for the serious reader, a serious, balanced, respectful history of Islam and Iran.

Here are some of the topics covered in this book:

- Does the Koran command Muslims to kill all non-Muslims?
- Are Muslim jihadists at war with Christians and Jews?
- Why is there a split between Sunni and Shia Muslims, and what is its importance today?
- What is Shia theology, how was it redefined by Iran's Supreme Leader, and how is Iran's Supreme Leader violating it?
- What is the importance of ancient Persian empires and Zoroastrianism to Iran today?
- How is today's Iran, recognized as one of the most corrupt governments in the world, controlled by a Constitution with no checks and balances?
- Why is there a big generational split in Iran?
- What kind of "regime change" does Iran need to restore the country's former glory?

Having written thousands of news articles analyzing Islam and Iran, I know what topics are of the greatest significance to readers and to today's world news. There are literally millions of topics that a book like this can include, but I've chosen the few dozen topics that will be most relevant for readers.

Furthermore, I've written this text in a respectful, balanced, non-ideological way that will be accessible to all points of view.

Some people may wonder whether it's possible or "appropriate" for a non-Muslim to write a book on Islam and Iran. I would argue the opposite. A Muslim author might be able to write a balanced treatment of Islam, but will suffer from the handicap that people within his own religion or sect may criticize him if he's totally non-ideological, and particularly if he discusses the very real controversies within Islam itself, such as the validity of the Koran and Hadith, polygamy and pedophilia in Islam, and whether the Koran commands all Muslims to kill all non-Muslims.

Since I'm not a Muslim, I'm able to describe Islam and Iran in a respectful, balanced, non-ideological way, but also describing the controversies within Islam that Muslims themselves feel obligated to avoid mentioning. In each case, I've been careful to describe both (or all) points of view in a balanced, non-ideological manner. I believe that this approach is valuable for Islam and the West.

I will admit in advance that I will be criticized for being biased against the current leadership in Iran. As an American, I cannot be indifferent to a leadership whose security forces massacre, jail, rape and torture peacefully protesting college students, nor one that fully supports a war criminal like Syria's president Bashar al-Assad. And of course I'm also biased against al-Qaeda, ISIS and other jihadist groups committing terror acts. But I've tried to limit my editorial comments to only cases where I have no choice.

I would describe the ordering of the sections of this book as "peeling an onion," starting with the most accessible political news about Iran over the last 20 years, and then proceeding step by step to the core of Iran's Shia Islam theology. A summary is as follows:

- Internal political conflicts in Iran, since the student riots of 1999 that challenged the entire legitimacy of the 1979 Great Islamic Revolution.
- A political history of Iran from the 1800s to the present, including the border wars with Britain and Russia, the Tobacco Revolt and Constitutional Revolution, the White Revolution and the Islamic Revolution. We show how each of these events flowed into the next one as new generations of Persians and Iranians grew up and replaced older generations.
- The great empires of Persian history, which still fill modern Iranians with pride even today.
- The conquest of Persia by Mohammed and the Islamic Arabs, and the Sunni-Shia split.

- Shia Islam's twelve infallible Imams, and development of Shia Islam Theology by Ayatollah Ruhollah Khomeini, through the "Guardianship of the Jurist." This involves a retelling of the history of Iran from 1800s to the present, but a theological history rather than a political history. This is the core of the onion, after all the layers have been peeled off.
- The future of Iran — the selection of a new Supreme Leader, and the inevitable regime change.

By the time we reach the end, we'll have circled back to the beginning, with what is hopefully a complete understanding of Iran today.

This book also draws on the methodologies provided by advanced generational theory as developed for 15 years on the web site GenerationalDynamics.com. These methodologies explain, for example, why there's a big generational split today between Iran's old government leaders versus young people, and they explain such things as the transition from Iran's Constitutional Revolution in 1905-09 to Iran's Islamic Revolution in 1979.

Chapter 2. Fact-checking this book

I've been as meticulous as possible in researching, collecting and presenting the facts in this book. Particular care has been taken in the meticulous researching of the history from roughly 630-680 AD on the details of the rise of Islam and the Sunni-Shia split.

In order to make it easier for readers, I've followed the technique of providing explicit birth and death years of many of the historical figures I write about — when those dates are known. These dates are useful for someone trying to learn more information by accessing other historical sources. Sometimes different people will have the same name in the same or different sources, and at other times the same person is referenced by different names in different sources, due to the vagaries of language transliteration. The things that appear to be most constant and reliable are the birth and death dates, and these dates can be used to match up the same people in different histories.

If a source references an Islamic date, then you can get an approximate date (plus or minus one year) in the Gregorian calendar using this formula: gregorian-year = (622 + .97*islamic-year). For example, the Islamic date 630 AH equals the Gregorian date 622+.97*630 = 1233 AD.

Much of the historical material in this book is extremely complex, and a lot of sources on the internet, even by people with expert knowledge of Islam, aren't experts on the details of all of it, and often get things wrong. Furthermore, when we're discussing issues like controversies in the creation of the Koran or validity of the Hadith, most Muslims would risk backlash and criticism for making any comment whatsoever on these subjects. There were times when I had to read and compare ten or twenty separate sources from multiple ideologies and points of view before I was feeling confident that I had gotten the facts 100% correct. This same problem also makes independent fact-checking of this material almost impossible, and so the author of this book invites comments from anyone who wishes to dispute any of these facts to let him know at the iran-book@GenerationalDynamics.com e-mail address. Any serious issues will be reported on the GenerationalDynamics.com web site.

Part II. Iran today and its internal conflicts

Chapter 3. Student protests of 1999

On July 9, 1999, thousands of students in Iran conducted anti-government protests. This event was almost as important as the 1979 Great Islamic Revolution itself, because for the first time since the 1979 revolution, with its society carefully cultivated to be unified in the holy pursuit of a life guided by charismatic Shia Islam, that Iran's society was shown to be bitterly split within itself, and that Shia's charismatic movement could fall apart as quickly as it had been formed.

There had been sporadic peaceful student demonstrations, triggered by a court decision to close a reformist newspaper, Salaam. But then on July 9, Iran unleashed its security thugs, and over the next week beat and tortured students, and arrested thousands.

The NY Times on July 11, 1999, explained what was happening just two days into the event:

> "A day after a violent police raid on a Teheran University dormitory, more than 10,000 students demonstrated here and in other Iranian cities today, chanting slogans against Government hard-liners and clashing at times with the police.

> The eruption of student anger, set off by a police crackdown on Friday that left at least 20 people hospitalized and 125 students jailed, rippled through the top levels of the Iranian Government today." [1]

The same NY Times report tells something else just as significant — that the student protests caused the first major splits in Iran's government since the 1979 Revolution. Even then, there were "moderate" and "hardline" factions in the government, and the then-current president, Mohammad Khatami, was considered a moderate, while the Supreme Leader Ayatollah Ali Khamenei was considered a hardliner.

Mohammad Khatami, a Reformist, had won a victory in the presidential elections of 1997, much to the shock and surprise of the hardliners. The hardliners reacted by sabotaging every attempt at reform, according to Khatami himself, by creating "a crisis every nine days" to break him. [101]

Khatami, representing the reformers, condemned the attacks on the protesting students in 1999. Supreme Leader Khamenei blamed the students, but decided to free the jailed students in order to keep the protests from getting worse. However, it didn't work:

> The nation's moderate Higher Education Minister, Mostafa Moin, offered to resign in protest against the university raid, which was apparently backed by some Islamic conservatives in the government.

> Further, seeking to appease the demonstrators, Iran's highest security body, led by the moderate President, Mohammad Khatami, condemned the police raid as 'intolerable' and vowed to dismiss the official who ordered it. ...

> [Khamenei's Supreme National Security Council] expressed sympathy with dozens of students wounded in the attacks and said those who had been arrested were now freed. ...

> Since those protests, which the riot police broke up by beating and arresting dozens of students, demands have increased to include thorough political reform and an end to the conservative grip on the main levers of state power, including the security forces.

> Among the students' demands today was the punishment of those responsible for what they said were the deaths of five students at the hands of the attackers. ...

> After the police raid overnight, some 10,000 students, joined by colleagues from other Teheran universities, rallied today and blocked a major thoroughfare near the campus.

> The rally began as supporters of President Khatami began a sit-in at the main campus, while many others marched from a dormitory complex several miles away. Some of the marchers covered their faces to disguise their identity.

> The students later marched across the capital to the Interior Ministry, and their ranks swelled with supporters. There were sporadic clashes with the police along the way.

> The protesters chanted slogans against the police chief, General Lotfian, whose officers had abetted the attack by the hardliners armed with tear gas, sticks and stones. Other slogans suggested that the students' patience was wearing thin as they

vented their anger at Iran's senior leadership for failing to protect them.

Early in the day, Teheran students and hard-liners, some armed with clubs, fought scattered battles. 'They are hitting the students, and the students are hitting back,' a witness said.

Demonstrators set fire to a motorcycle belonging to the vigilantes, identified as members of the Ansar-e Hezbollah, a group with shadowy ties to the Islamic establishment.

A spokesman for the students, who was arrested and later released, told reporters that he and his classmates had been 'physically and mentally tortured during detention.'" [1]

These protests occurred 20 years after the 1979 Great Islamic Revolution. This was the first time in the history of the Islamic Republic of Iran that a generation of young people who grew up after the revolution were old enough to make their voices heard, and their voices directly contradicted the violent, oppressive demands of Iran's hardline "revolutionary" government.

Chapter 4. More protests during the generational awakening of Iran's college students

Iran's 1999 student riots triggered a generational split that is not unique to Iran. Those old enough to remember the 1960s and 1970s will recall that there were similar anti-government demonstrations in America and Europe, although they weren't met with the same violence as the Iranian protesters received.

From the point of view of generational theory, these kinds of demonstrations always begin around 20 years after the end of a particularly large, bloody war — World War II in the case of America, and the 1979 civil war in the case of Iran. What always happens is that when the war ends, the survivors do everything possible to make sure that nothing like it happens again. This often means making undesirable compromises or imposing stifling rules on society.

After 20 years pass, a new generation has grown up with no personal memory of the war, and their voices are heard through objecting to the compromises and rules that their parents had set up to prevent a new war. This results in what is popularly called a "generation gap" or a "generational split." In generational theory it's called a "generational awakening," because the first generation growing up after a generational crisis war begins to make itself heard.

In America in the 1960s, these demonstrations became antiwar protests, anti-discrimination protests, pro-environment protests, and sexual freedom protests that were characterized by events where boys burned their draft cards while girls burned their bras.

In 2002, NY Times columnist Thomas Friedman described the generational split in Iran at that time. He was writing on June 6, 2002, just before the third anniversary of the 1999 protests:

> "Iran has the bomb. I know. I found it.
>
> No, no not that bomb. This bomb is hiding in plain sight — in high schools, universities and coffee houses. It is a bomb that is ticking away under Iranian society, and over the next decade it will explode in ways that will change the face of this Islamic Republic. It's called here, for short, "The Third Generation."

The first generation of Iranian revolutionaries overthrew the Shah in 1979 and founded the Islamic Republic. They are now old, gray and increasingly tired, a clerical regime clinging to power more by coercion than by any popular acceptance of their plan to Islamize all aspects of Iranian life. The second generation came of age during the 1980's Iran-Iraq war, which left 286,000 Iranians dead and 500,000 injured. This is a lost generation, deflated and quiescent.

The third generation are those Iranians from 16 to 30 who have come of age entirely under Islamic rule. They never knew the Shah's despotism. They have known only the aya- tollahs'. There are now 18 million of them — roughly a third of Iran's population — and they include 2 million university students and 4 million recent university grads. ...

Where this Third Generation wants to go is already apparent. While some of them are religious conservatives, most are not. They are young, restless, modern-looking and often unem- ployed, because there are not enough good jobs. They are connected to the world via the Internet or satellite dishes — and they like what they see. They want the good life, a good job, more individual freedom and more connections with the outside world — and they are increasingly angry that they don't have those things. They embrace Islam, but they don't want it to occupy every corner of their lives. ...

This Third Generation hoped President Khatami's reformist candidacy would satisfy those aspirations, but he proved to be a bust, unwilling to confront the conservatives. No matter. The Third Generation will eventually find a new political horse to ride and, when it does, Iran will change — with or without the ayatollahs' blessings." [3]

Friedman's description of these 18 million people in the "third generation," 16-30 years old, did not make Iran's hardliners very happy.

In another column, Friedman wrote that a large number of people — presumably young people — who were pro-American:

"Quick quiz: Which Muslim Middle East country held spon- taneous candlelight vigils in sympathy with Americans after Sept. 11? Kuwait? No. Saudi Arabia? No. Iran? Yes. You got it! You win a free trip to Iran. And if you come you'll discover not only a Muslim country where many people were sincerely sympathetic to America after Sept. 11, but a country where so many people on the street are now talking about — and hoping for — a reopening of relations with America that the ruling hard-liners had to take the unprecedented step two weeks ago of making it illegal for anyone to speak about it in public." [2]

For Iran's hardliners, it was bad enough that Friedman described a "third generation" of young post-war Iranians who were angry at their hardline government leaders, but writing that they sympathize with America and like America was too much for the hardliners. Iran accused Friedman of espionage, suggested that he was an Israeli or American spy, and banned him from returning to Iran.

So let's do some simple math. Those 18 million people in Friedman's "third generation" were aged 16-30 in 2002, and today they are now 34-48 years old. The vicious treatment that they received in 1999 and the years after may have forced them to shut their mouths, but it didn't change their minds. They're now moving into positions of power, while the old geezer hardliner survivors of the 1979 civil war, including Supreme Leader Seyed Ali Khamenei, born 1939, and now 79 years old, are not going to be around forever.

Chapter 5. The 2009 election and the Green movement

When Mohammed Khatami was president, he was a big disappointment to the peacefully protesting college students in 1999, because even though he was a Reformist, he was unwilling or unable to prevent the massive bloody slaughter and torture that the hardliners inflicted on them.

Although there were additional protests throughout the 2000s, the next protest that was large enough to be a threat to the government occurred after the 2009 presidential election. The Reformist candidate was Mir Hossein Mousavi, while the hardline candidate was Mahmoud Ahmadinejad, who was running for re-election.

Opposition supporters claimed massive election fraud, after the Interior Ministry announced an overwhelming victory for Ahmadinejad, with 62.6% of the vote, against 33.75% for Mousavi. The turnout was a record 85% of Iran's 46.2 million eligible voters.

Opposition leaders pointed out that polls had indicated a very close election, and Mousavi had a good chance to win if turnout was high. The turnout was in fact extremely high, with millions of new voters, but the announced election results seemed to imply that all the new voters voted for Ahmadinejad. This appeared very unlikely, in view of the huge election rallies for Mousavi in the preceding days. Whatever the truth is about whether election fraud has occurred, the perception was that it HAS occurred, and this infuriated supporters of Mousavi and other opposition and reform leaders.

The violence that followed was bloody and massive. Largely peaceful street protests by hundreds of thousands of mostly young people occurred in Iran's main cities and provincial capitals, including Tehran, Tabriz, Isfahan and Shiraz. They were met with unrestrained violence by the police and security forces. Dozens were killed, and 4,000 people were jailed. The police particularly targeted journalists and other government critics with widespread torture, beatings, and threats against family members. [102]

The immense street demonstrations came to be known as the "Green Movement." The Green Movement of 2009 was firmly rooted in the reformist political movement, symbolized by former president Mohammad Khatami, the would-be president Mousavi and other prominent politicians who advocated greater margins of freedom and opening to the West. That gave the protests a base and organization able to mobilize massive numbers. It also gave the hardliners a set of easy targets. The leadership was quickly arrested, prosecuted and imprisoned, resulting in the end of the Green Movement, in any formal sense. [102]

New widespread protests occurred in December 2017. They were smaller than the 2009 protests, but they were considered more dangerous to the regime because they were so spontaneous and unfocused. The 2009 protests had leaders and demanded specific reforms, within the existing constitutional framework. The 2017 protests had no leaders, and spread spontaneously, beginning with a protest in the city of Mashad against the price of eggs, and then spreading quickly to other cities. [101]

The 2017 protests did not demand specific reforms. Instead, they demanded the end of the entire regime. They demanded an end to corruption, an end to support for foreign wars, including an end to support for the war in Syria, and end to support for terror group Hezbollah, an end to support for Palestinians fighting Israel, and an end to the position of Supreme Leader. [107]

A lot of people have been calling for regime change in Iran, and see these protests as the path to a quick change. We'll discuss regime change a great deal more in this book, in the context of Shia theology. But here, two points must be made.

First, street protests do not mean that regime change is imminent. To the contrary, the street protests may cause the regime to take steps to reduce the danger of regime change. At any rate, regime change may not occur for years or even decades.

Second, a new regime may not be any better than the current one. Iran has a history of jailing, torturing, raping and killing political enemies. That's what Iran was like during the regime of the Shah of Iran, and that's what Iran has been like since the 1979 revolution. A new regime has a good chance of being exactly the same.

Part III. Iran in the 19th-20th centuries

You can't understand a society or nation without understanding some of its history, especially the things in its history that it's proud of. For example, if you want to understand America today, then you have to at least start by understanding the Revolutionary War (1776-1782) and the American Civil War (1861-65).

Similarly, if you want to understand Iran today, then you have to at least start by understanding the Russo-Persian wars (1804-1828) the Anglo-Persian war (1856-1857), and especially the Constitutional Revolution (1905-1909).

It's hard to overestimate the importance of the Constitutional Revolution to the thinking and behavior of the people and government of Iran today, because it affects almost every popular protest and every government action.

So we're going to describe the Constitutional Revolution in three steps:

- The first step is the history of Iran's border wars in the 1800s, resulting in disastrous and humiliating losses for Iran to Russia and Britain.
- The second step is the world history of constitutions, and how they became globally important, especially after America's Constitution was ratified in 1789.
- The third step merges the last two. We show how public disillusionment with repeated humiliating failures in Iran's border wars led the people to demand a Constitution that would control government excesses. This led to a major civil war known as the Constitutional Revolution.

Once we understand how Iran arrived at the Constitutional Revolution, we can then see how it led to the Great Islamic Revolution, and with today's public dissatisfaction with the current government's excesses — many of which are clear violations of Iran's current constitution.

In the chapters after that, we'll go deeper into Iran's history, back to the great Persian empires of ancient times. We'll be particularly interested in the difference between Shia Muslims and Sunni Muslims, and why they've been at war for fifteen centuries.

Chapter 6. Iran in the 1800s

Europe was in turmoil in the 1800s, first because of the Napoleonic wars, and later because of the various wars of national unification in the 1850s-70s, such as the wars of unification for Germany and Italy.

Iran was also in turmoil in the 1800s, and for much the same reason as Europe — nations were struggling to define themselves and their boundaries. There was no United Nations or other international organizations defining these boundaries. Nations claimed whatever borders they wanted, and in the case of disagreement, there was no United Nations Security Council to rule on who was right. The only way to resolve the question of who was right to was to have a border war. And Iran had plenty of border wars in the 1800s.

The greatest empire of ancient times was the Achaemenid Persian Empire (550–330 BC). To the West, it extended as far as Egypt and Anatolia (Turkey). To the North, it included Azerbaijan and parts of the Caucasus, as well as parts of Central Asia. To the East, it extended through today's Afghanistan and Pakistan, all the way to what is now the border of India.

Of course, Persia had lost much of that empire by the 1800s, and many people at that time had dreams of restoring some or all of the Achaemenid Empire. The attempts to do so were disastrous.

For centuries, the great battles over the Caucasus had been between the Ottomans (Turkey) and Russia, between a great Sunni Muslim civilization and a great Orthodox Christian civilization. As Shia Muslims, the Iranians were not really part of either of those civilizations, and instead became collateral damage in the wars between them.

So in the early 1800s, Russia was expanding from the north into the Caucasus Mountains, and Iran went to war to stop them. The war was a disaster for Iran, and resulted in the Treat of Gulistan/Golestan in 1813, in which Iran recognized Russia's annexation of Georgia and ceded to Russia most of the north Caucasus region. [32]

After that disastrous loss, there was a strong public outcry against Russia, and a surge in jihadist literature "to protect the lands of Islam," led by Mirza Abbas Buzurg, a vizier (minister of state) of the shah, and also the father of the founder of the Bahai offshoot of Shia Islam. [37]

Mirza Buzurg explained that the Iranian people were obligated to pursue this jihad for two reasons — to reverse Russia's conquest of

Muslim countries by the Orthodox Christian Russians, and to obey the shah:

> "It is clear to all the Muslims and to the mature public that in the past few years the Russian infidels have seized upon the countries of the Muslims and are in the process of conquering the kingdoms of Islam. ... On the whole of the Iranian public it is obligatory to obey that excellency [Fath Ali Shah], who is the king of Islam and [thus] the chief commander to obey in this regard, and to follow the Neib al-Saltanah, who is in charge of the matter of jihad." [35]

From the point of view of generational theory, when a country enters a "generational Crisis era," there are two effects on the population: the people become increasingly nationalistic, and they become increasingly xenophobic. Mirza's statements appealed to both emotions, by stoking incitement against the Russian infidels, raising hawkish anger in the public, and leading to a new war.

Unfortunately, emotions don't necessarily turn into victories. Iran's next war with Russia was even more disastrous than the previous one. In the 1828 Treaty of Torkamanchay (Turkmanchai, Turkomanchay, Torkama Cay), Russia acquired a number of additional conquered territories, including Georgia and parts of Armenia. Furthermore, Iran incurred enormous debt, including war payments to Russia. This was the climax of the generational crisis war with the Russians, and it left Iran's population with no interest in further wars through the end of the century.

As devastating as the Persian-Russian wars were, they did produce one good outcome: the boundaries of Iran to the northwest were pretty much settled, and reaffirmed by treaty. There would be no more hawkish desire for border wars.

In the 1840s, a border commission was set up with representatives from the Ottomans, Persians, Russians and British. The objective was to set up firm boundaries, and bring an end to border wars for all time. Not surprisingly, there was little agreement among the participants, and therefore the commission had little success, and could not come up with more than a few vague statements that didn't settle anything. Even where there might have been success, there is always the problem that herder tribes are constantly moving around, and refugee populations also frequently move in order to escape discrimination and massacres by regional governments and leaders. (This is no different than the problems we're seeing today, especially in Africa and the Mideast.)

The 1850s brought the Crimean War to the Ottomans and Russians. That war was a disaster to both sides, so it did little to settle boundary issues. By 1869, the British-led boundary commission had drawn up a map that neither the Persians nor the Ottomans honored, but it served the purpose of making it clear what the differences were. That left the boundaries between Iran, Turkey and other countries unsettled until they were settled by World War I.

That's the story of Iran's eastern boundaries. The fights over Iran's western boundaries were equally chaotic and equally disastrous.

After Iran's disastrous loss to Russia, culminating in the 1828 Treaty of Torkamanchay, Iran in 1831 began its attempt to reassert control over Herat, a large region in western Afghanistan on the border with Iran. In this case, it was the British colonists in India who were opposing Iran's land claims.

As an aside, it's worth noting in passing that this was not a good time for the British army in Asia. The Crimean War had been a disaster for both Russia and Turkey, but it had also been disastrous for the British. The most enduring British memory of the war is told in "The Charge of the Light Brigade" by Victorian poet Alfred Lord Tennyson, describing how 600 British soldiers were sent to their deaths by bungling commanders on October 25, 1854. [38]

Britain was also heavily occupied in colonial India, where anti-British unrest among both the Hindus and Muslims was increasing, and what was about to occur was the the 1857 rebellion (India's First War of Independence), a war that lasted over two years and resulted in hundreds of thousands of death.

It was into this febrile atmosphere that Iran launched what was to be the Anglo-Persian war. After numerous false starts, Herat fell to the Persians at the end of October, 1856. The British were concerned that Iranian control of Herat could create a weakness that would lead to a Russian attack on India, Britain's colony. In December, 1856, Britain declared war on Persia, leading to yet another debacle for the Persians. Peace was officially achieved with the Treaty of Paris, which was ratified by all parties on May 2, 1857. Terms were extremely humiliating to Persia, which was obliged to relinquish all claims over Herat and Afghanistan, while Britain was to serve as arbiter in any disputes between Persia and the Afghan states. [39]

That war settled Iran's eastern boundaries. Just as borders to the west of Iran would remain relatively settled until World War I, borders to the east of Iran would remain relatively settled until World War II.

At the beginning of the 1800s, Iran's people might have dreamed of restoring the glory of historical Persian empires that had stretched from Egypt to the border with India. At the end of the 1800s, Iran's dreams had been shattered in humiliation, and they were demanding accountability from their leaders.

Chapter 7. History of Constitutions

This chapter is a side trip. We want to describe Iran's Constitutional Revolution of 1905-1909, and its enormous effect on today's Iran, but first we want to discuss what a Constitution is, and why it's important.

We've described Iran's disastrous border wars in the 1800s. By the end of the 1800s, these led to enormous public dissatisfaction with Iran's leaders, and demands for an Iranian Constitution that would control the excesses of Iran's government.

Let's look at the development of constitutions throughout history. From time immemorial, ordinary peasants and workers needed protection from the excesses of their kings, queens, and other leaders. But they rarely got such protection, because leaders had absolute power, and even owned the people they led, as if they were inanimate objects. If a leader needed money, he could raise taxes without getting anyone's approval. If he wanted to fight a war, he could raise an army. If he needed sex, he could grab any passing maid (to use the phrase from the Broadway play Camelot).

Traditionally, there's really only one thing that can control an abusive monarch, and that's a popular revolt by the people.

It's true that "all experience hath shewn that mankind are more disposed to suffer, while evils are sufferable than to right themselves by abolishing the forms to which they are accustomed," as stated in the American Declaration of Independence, but revolts take place when the evils become insufferable.

History has shown that these kinds of popular revolts tend to take place at reasonably regular intervals, the length of a human lifespan. A popular revolt is usually a civil war where people end up fighting, torturing, raping and killing their former friends and neighbors, so once such a period of violence finally ends, the survivors will do everything possible, including making many compromises, to make sure that it doesn't happen again. When the survivors all die off, 60-70 years later, then there's a new popular revolt, and history repeats.

This brings us to the concept of a "constitution," a form of law designed to limit the powers of the monarch.

Going back to ancient times, the West is most familiar with Roman law, and the Arab world is most familiar with Sharia law (which came centuries after Roman law, and was largely based on Roman law). But Roman Law and Sharia Law generally do not limit the monarch. They have to do with the rules that ordinary citizens live by — rules for marriage and divorce, rules for resolving disputes with your neighbor, and administrative rules such as the requirements to pay taxes.

Laws that limited the powers of monarchs did not exist in ancient times. In Europe, the first such law was the Magna Carta, signed in June 1215 by English King John and his barons, who forced it on him after several military failures in northern France. The Magna Carta established the principle that the king is subject to the same feudal laws as everyone else.

On April 13, 1655, France's King Louis XIV supposedly said "L'état c'est moi!" or "I am the state," to express supremacy over, and contempt for, the French Parliament. Most historians believe that the story is apocryphal, but it does represent the view at the time that the King had absolute power.

A related story is the War of the Spanish Succession. This was the "world war" of the time, fought in Europe in 1701-1714. The war was triggered by the death of the King of Spain. When his will was read, it turned out that he bequeathed Spain to the grandson of the King of France. Bequeathing Spain to French royalty completely unraveled existing European peace treaties that had been signed in 1648 after the Thirty Years War, and the War of Spanish Succession began. This story shows how, in the days before constitutional law, countries and populations were objects to get bought, sold and bequeathed in wills.

So there were scattered attempts through the centuries at laws to limit the powers of monarchs, but everything changed in 1789, with the ratification of the Constitution of the United States, and the related document, the Bill of Rights.

The U.S. Constitution is thought to be the oldest written constitution still in use today. It defines three co-equal branches of government, including a leader called the "president," and it defines and severely limits the powers of each of the three branches.

After the U.S. Constitution began rather successfully being used in the actual process of governing, the idea of a written constitution became rather fashionable in many countries during the 1800s. Although the US Constitution was rarely if ever simply copied verbatim, it did provide a template to be used for constitutions of many forms of government.

The first attempts were performed in France as the French Revolution was launched in 1789. This is not surprising, as France and America were allied against England in America's Revolutionary War, and would be again in America's War of 1812. So the French revolutionaries, inspired by America's constitution, first tried a written constitution in 1791, then again in 1793, and then again in 1795. In each case, the new constitution represented the latest ideas of whoever had just taken power in France's civil war. [95]

Finally, with Napoleon Bonaparte in full power, a new French constitution was announced in 1800. Although amended many times, the constitution was widely admired. Jean-Antoine Chaptal, one of Napoleon's ministers, was pleased that it limited some of Napoleon's powers: "Truly it is difficult to conceive of a constitution which offers more guarantees for the rights of the people. It is difficult to leave less to the fiat of the head of the government. The limits of power are clear and unambiguous." [95]

With Napoleon's empire collapsing in 1814, Norway was the next to adopt a written constitution. It was founded on principles of the sovereignty of the people, the separation of powers, and human rights. It established three branches of government: Executive power, vested in the King in Council, as well as legislative and judicial branches. [93]

The next major constitution to be inspired by the US Constitution was Belgium's, adopted in 1831 as Belgium was declaring independence. It also specified three major branches of government, but recognized the King as the supreme authority over the other branches. [94]

As these examples illustrate, the 1800s witnessed in America and Europe an enormous change in the public view of their leaders. While kings and monarchs formerly had absolute power, as if they actually owned their subjects (which they did in some cases), the American constitution showed people the mechanism that would put restraints on a leader, and the French revolution showed how a constitution could be imposed on the leader, even against his will.

Chapter 8. Concessions, Capitulations and the Tobacco Revolt (1890-92)

The idea of a constitution spread fairly rapidly through European countries, but did not reach Iran for a while because Iran was fairly isolated from Europe. It took much of the 1800s for Iran to become aware of the advantages of European "civilization," and the mechanism that was used to integrate Iran with Europe was the "capitulatory system" — a system whose ultimate rejection as "Western imperialism" led to Iran's Constitutional Revolution, as we'll see.

8.1. The Capitulatory System of the Middle East (1500s-1900s)

The "capitulatory system" of the Middle East was developed starting in the 1500s during the rise of the Ottoman empire (Turkey). A capitulation was an agreement between two countries to permit one country to grant various concessions to another country.

For example, the Ottoman government wanted to promote commercial exchanges with the West, so that the Ottomans and the Europeans could buy and sell goods with another. In today's world, we have all kinds of laws and institutions that control trade between countries — the World Trade Organization, tariff systems, NAFTA, various free trade agreements, and so forth. But none of that existed in the 1500s.

So in 1536, Ottoman ruler Suleyman the Magnificent granted a "capitulation" to France's ruler King Francis I, an agreement that specified greatly reduced tariff rates between the two countries, and that made French merchants immune from Ottoman law. [41]

The 1536 capitulation remained in place for over two centuries, and provided the mechanism for greatly expanded trade and commerce between the Ottomans and the Europeans. However, it eventually became unpopular, and by the 1700s, the capitulation system was viewed by many Ottomans as giving western Europe a distinct military and commercial advantage over the Ottoman Empire. The Anglo-Turkish Commercial Convention and the treaty of Balta Liman in 1838 ended the traditional system of capitulations for the Ottoman empire, and began the system of bilateral commercial treaties that are the subject of many news stories today. [41]

The capitulation system was used by the Ottomans to expand trade and commerce with Europe, and starting in the 1800s it was used by Iran for the same reasons. The Persian Qajar government in the 1800s granted capitulations to Britain and Russia, but not just for commercial reasons.

After Persia's disastrous and humiliating losses to the Russians and British, resulting in the 1828 Treaty of Torkamanchay and the 1857 Treaty of Paris, capitulations were forced on the Persians that required loss of territory and payment of monies. They required numerous other concessions as well, including monopolies, contracts, and licenses to British and Russian citizens and companies to carry on specific economic activities on Persian territory.

Economic concessions fell into three major categories: public utilities, financial enterprises, and exploration for and exploitation of natural resources. Whether the concessions were imposed or not, they did confer some benefits to Iran. For example, the British established and operates telegraph lines in Persia, opened the Karun river to international navigation in 1888, and, between 1890 and 1913, constructed and operated roads and railroads in the southern and western provinces of the country. [40]

Similar concessions were granted to Russian interests, including, in 1889, the right to navigate Persian rivers flowing into the Caspian Sea, to anchor in the Anzali lagoon, and to build depots and roads between Pirbazar on the Caspian coast and Tehran. Other concessions permitted the construction of roads and railroads, and the construction of an oil pipeline from Anzali to Rast in 1911. [40]

Taken as a whole, Persian concessions encouraged foreign trade, commercialization of agriculture, contacts with the West, and gradual incorporation of the country into the world economy. On the other hand, they were discriminatory to Persian traders and were often resented by Persian merchants and the intelligentsia, who recognized in them the increasing domination of the country by colonial powers and blamed them for its continued "backwardness." [40]

8.2. The Tobacco Revolt (1890-92)

This discontent with concessions led to the Tobacco Revolt (1890-92), an almost unprecedented event in Iranian history, because the public revolted peacefully for a clear and well-defined purpose.

Whereas traditional Iranian rebellions, like rebellions in other countries, had the purpose of overthrowing an "unjust" ruler, to replace him with a "just" ruler, this revolt began with the specific purpose of forcing the leader to reverse a policy decision, namely a concession to Britain over tobacco. [33]

The tobacco concession granted a monopoly on both the purchase and sale of tobacco within Persia to an English company for a period of fifty years. During this period the Qajar rulers of Iran would annually receive 15,000 pounds and 25 percent of the profit generated by the concession arrangement. The agreement stated all producers were required to inform the concessionaires of the amount of crop that they produced annually and then sell their entire crop to the British company. All tobacco merchants were required to seek permits from the concessionaires and immediately pay, in cash, for all tobacco they obtained. [42]

The tobacco concession struck at the heart of Iran's culture. At this time, nearly everyone in Iran, both men and women, used tobacco products, as they gathered to smoke and drink coffee. The tobacco merchants felt their livelihood threatened, and enlisted the help of other bazaar merchants to organize anti-government protests. A religious cleric by the name of Mirza Mohammed Hassan Husseini Shirazi (1815-1896) issued a fatwa supporting the protests. Even though this fatwa was later thought to have been forged, the fatwa had huge significance in both the political development of Iran and also the development of Shia theology, as we'll discuss in later chapters. [42]

The fatwa convinced many government supporters to switch sides and support the protesters. In the northern regions of Iran under Russian influence, including today's Azerbaijan, support for the protests was strong because the monopoly had been granted to the British, locking out the Russians. [42]

The debate sounds very modern, as illustrated by one of many published letters:

> "A merchant from Qazvin writes: "By what laws does the government sell our national rights to foreign racketeers? These rights, according to both the principles of Islam and traditional laws of Iran, belong to the people of our country. These rights are the means of our livelihood. The government, however, barters the Moslem property to the unbelievers. By what law? Have the people of Iran died that the government is auctioning away their inheritance?"
>
> Dear Merchant, the government has mistaken our inaction for our death. It is time for the mujtaheds and other knowledge-

able persons to arise and save the people of Iran. We propose two simple remedies to save Iran: law and more law. You may well ask, "where will this law come from?" The answer is again simple: the shah should call at once one hundred mujtaheds and other learned persons of the country into a national consultative assembly (majles-i shawra-yi melli); and this assembly should have full authority to formulate laws that would initiate social progress." [42]

The Shah was forced to rescind the tobacco concession, but some protests continued, with the worst occurring in Tehran a week later, where ten people were killed. The Shah tried to defend his prerogatives in a letter to a political advisor:

"Do you know that no one can rise against the government? Do you know that if — God forbid — there was no government, those same Babis of Tehran would cut off your heads? Do you not know that if the government were not there your wives and children would fall into the hands of the Russian Cossacks, the Ottoman soldiers, the English army, the Afghans, or the Turkomans? It is a pity that you, with your knowledge and intelligence, should give your reason into the hands of a few talaba (students of religious schools), ruffians and scum of the city and act according to their desires." [42]

The Tobacco Revolt was a major event in Iranian history, with implications far beyond the income of tobacco merchants. The protests were not about replacing one ruler with another, but rather about the law: whether a leader can be controlled by the law, and whether a leader is above the law, questions that are still relevant today.

Chapter 9. Iran's Constitutional Revolution (1905-09)

The Tobacco Revolt provided a template to the public in 1905, when there were protests over an increase in the price of sugar. The government blamed the sugar merchants, and several sugar merchants were beaten and tortured. A leading preacher and radical constitutionalist, Seyyed Jamal al-Din Isfahani attacked the government from the pulpit, leading to public protests, especially from students, merchants and shopkeepers. [33]

The following is an excerpt from one of Isfahani's sermons:

> "People! Nothing would develop your country other than subjection to law, observation of law, preservation of law, respect for law, implementation of the law, and again law, and once again law. Children must from childhood read and learn at schools that no sin in religion and the shari'eh is worse than opposing the law...Observing religion means law, religion means law, Islam, the Koran, mean God's law. My dear man, qanun, qanun. Children must understand, women must understand, that the ruler is law and law alone, and no one's rule is valid but that of the law. The parliament is the protector of law...The legislative assembly and legislature is the assembly which makes law, the sultan is the head of the executive which implements the law. The soldier is defender of the law, the police is defender of the law, justice means law, riches means implementing the law, the independence of the monarchy means rules of the law. In a word, the development of the country, the foundation of every nationality, and the solidarity of every nation arises from the implementation of the law."

I find it quite remarkable that this repeated invocation of the law could be the key to stir the emotions of the public, but it shows how thoroughly the public had become convinced that law could be used as a tool to control injustices by the élite. This included not just merchants and shopkeepers, but even members of the élite — clerics, tribal leaders, state officials, royals, and even Qajar clansmen — united by openly despising the system of arbitrary law, and by the fantasy that invocation of the law would make them free. [33]

By January 1906, the Shah [Muzaffar al-Din Shah Qajar] agreed to the public demands, including formation of a house of justice, or consultative assembly. The Shah did not follow up on his promises, leading to a confrontation involving a group of clerics and their students in which a student was killed. This triggered wider protests, with over 12,000 protesters demanding the formation of a majlis, or parliament. The first majlis convened in October 1906 and set about the task of writing a constitution. An ailing Shah decreed the document they produced into law in December 1906, a few days before his death. In October 1907 the new king signed the Supplementary Fundamental Law. Together, the two documents formed the core of the Iranian Constitution. [43]

Mohammad Ali Shah Qajar, the Shah of Persia, [the son of Muzaffar al-Din Shah Qajar], who ascended the throne in January 1907 was against the constitution of 1906 ratified during regime of his father Mozzafar-al-Din Shah. Iran was still under occupation of Russian forces in the north and British forces in the south, and both the Russian and British forces supported the Shah in opposing the constitution and the Majlis. On June 23, 1908, Russia's Cossack Brigade shelled and plundered the parliament building, executing several constitutionalist leaders. The Shah and the Cossack Brigade ruled until July 1909, when pro-Constitution forces marched from Iran's province of Azerbaijan to Tehran, defeating the Cossacks, deposing the Shah, and re-establishing the constitution. [44]

That was the climax of Iran's Constitutional Revolution. So finally, over a century after America's written constitution and the French Revolution and its imposition of law, Iran had officially become a country ruled by law, not by leaders who are above the law.

In the Fall of 1911, Russia, with the support of England, gave the majlis an ultimatum that would essentially nullify Iran's independence. Russian troops brutally killed some of the leading constitutionalists and stormed the Majlis. However, the Majlis and the Constitution were retained. [43]

Chapter 10. Iran after the Constitutional Revolution (1909-53)

10.1. Iran during World War I

World War I followed. Americans and Europeans tend to think of World War I as less important than World War II, but for the Mideast, World War I was cataclysmic. In particular, it saw the destruction of Tsarist Russia and the rise of the Russian empire and the Soviet Union, and it saw the destruction of the Ottoman Empire and the rise of secularist Turkey.

Iran's problem is that it's so centrally located that it can never be ignored. Iran tried to remain neutral, but ended up as a battleground for Russian, Turkish, and British troops. In February 1921, an officer from Persia's Cossacks Brigade, Reza Khan, marched into Tehran and seized power. [45]

By 1925, the Qajar Dynasty, which had ruled Iran since 1785, was deposed, and young 22-year-old Reza Khan, now Reza Shah, became the first Shah in the new Pahlavi Dynasty. The 1930s was an awakening era for Iran, and the young Reza Shah wanted to modernize the country for the 20th century. One of his most significant changes was to recognize that the population of the country consisted of a lot more than just Persians, so he he changed the official name of the country from Persia to Iran, a name that had been used unofficially for centuries.

The cornerstone of Reza Shah's economic reforms was the Trans-Iranian Railroad, linking the Persian Gulf to the Caspian Sea, completed in 1938. Reza Shah also initiated reforms in the areas of education and law, which were historically the domain of the clergy. Compulsory education for all Iranians was decreed, and hundreds of schools were built. In 1934, the University of Tehran was established. [43]

10.2. Iran during World War II

As in the case of World War I, Iran tried to stay neutral in World War II. Reza Shah had always tried to maintain good relations with many countries — Britain, the Soviet Union, Germany, France, Italy, and others. However, that obviously became impossible after the war began, and Iran was forced to choose sides whether it wanted to or not.

There were three major issues that prevented Iran from maintaining the neutrality it wanted to maintain:

- As in the case of World War I, Iran was just too centrally located to be ignored by any of the World War II combatants.
- The newly opened Trans-Iranian Railroad, linking the Persian Gulf to the Caspian Sea, became an extremely valuable transport mechanism, as recognized by the British and the Soviets. In 1942, the United States, which was an ally of Britain and the Soviets, sent a military force to Iran to help maintain and operate sections of the railroad.
- The Anglo-Iranian Oil company had become a major oil exporter.

With American forces in control, this resulted in the collapse of Reza Shah's government in 1942. They permitted Reza Shah's son, Mohammad Reza Shah Pahlavi to succeed to the throne. This is the person who became known to America and the world as "The Shah of Iran," until he was deposed by the 1979 revolution. [46] </li>

10.3. Anglo-Iranian Oil company nationalized, and 1953 CIA coup

At this point in describing the history of Iran, an explanation must be provided. If you seek out histories of Iran prior to WW II, they're all mostly in agreement, possibly emphasizing different things. But after the nationalization of Anglo-Iranian Oil and the 1953 CIA coup, most online histories are wildly ideological and political, written by journalists, analysts and politicians who often have no clue what was going on in the world either then or today, but in each case nonetheless absolutely certain that his particular left-wing or right-wing ideology explains everything.

So, for example, you might have one history claiming that the CIA coup was the end of democracy in Iran and the cause of the 1979 revolution, and you might have another history claim that the CIA coup prevented Iran from becoming a communist nation controlled by the Soviets, which would have resulted in an Iranian revolution much sooner.

I use a particular methodology for analyzing history. Generational theory is a completely non-ideological methodology that ignores the fatuous ideological and political claims illustrated above, and identifies the factors that lead to "great events," like revolutions. This methodology has been illustrated in thousands of articles on my web site, GenerationalDynamics.com, and has been overwhelmingly successful and accurate.

In analyzing older events, a generational theory analysis usually coincides pretty closely with most mainstream politicians. So, for example, I've been giving a generational analysis of the Russo-Persian and Anglo-Persian wars of the 1800s, and the Consitutional Revolution of the early 1900s. These events occurred so long ago that today's polemicists have never heard of them, and so rarely festoon them with fatuous ideological constructs.

But starting with the nationalization of Anglo-Iranian Oil we have events that are within the living memory of many politicians, polemicists and ideologues, so they feel free to attach even the most ridiculous meanings to the events.

What generational theory does is to analyze modern events in the same way that it analyzes events in the distant past. The generational methodology identifies the facts that are most significant, and uses those in the analyses and narratives.

Now, it's a core principle of generational theory that, even in a dictatorship, major decisions are made by masses of people, by generations of people. The attitudes of politicians are irrelevant, except insofar as they represent the attitudes of the people. The reason that generational theory works is that population generations are almost completely predictable, irrespective of what politicians want.

An example that I like to use is that World War II and the Jewish genocide would have occurred with or without Adolf Hitler, and would not have been prevented by killing Hitler in 1935, as some historians have claimed. Many histories have shown that the seeds of the Jewish genocide and WW II were planted in the minds of Europeans centuries earlier, long before the rise of Hitler.

So from the point of view of generational theory, the 1979 revolution would have occurred whether the CIA had intervened in 1953 or not. Those who claim otherwise would at the very least have to explain why the revolution didn't occur in 1954 or 1955 or 1965 or 1970.

Generational theory explains that the 1979 Great Islamic Revolution occurred at around the time the generations of survivors of the Constitutional Revolution had all disappeared (retired or died).

So with that background, let's now summarize the important facts about what happened in the early 1950s.

In 1901, British financier William Knox D'Arcy had signed a concession (contract) with Iran giving his company exclusive rights for 60 years to explore, obtain and market oil and natural gas. As oil was discovered, and as the British Royal Navy took interest, D'Arcy's contract turned into the Anglo-Persian Oil Company (APOC), later renamed to Anglo-Iranian Oil Company (AIOC). [50]

As the dust settled at the end of World War II, Iranian workers at AIOC began demanding higher wages and better working conditions. This led to a new agreement between Britain and Iran, the Gass-Golsha'yan (Golsa'ian) agreement, reached on July 17, 1949, increasing Iran's royalties on oil extraction. It became a major political issue when the Majlis (parliament) refused to ratify the agreement, and it was held over into the new Majlis elections. [50]

This led to the rise of Dr. Mohammad Mosaddeq, a prominent member of Tehran's ruling élite since the start of the century. In the elections for the 1950 Majlis, he made the oil agreement a major campaign issue, and became chairman of the committee that dealt with the agreement. Mosaddeq rejected the AIOC agreement, initially favoring a different oil company, and then favoring full nationalization of all of AIOC's properties. When the Prime Minister recommended against nationalization he was assassinated. The Majlis in March of 1951 enacted the legislation nationalizing the petroleum industry, and public demonstrations forced as the Shah to appoint Mossadeq as the new prime minister. [49]

The British oil companies retaliated against the nationalization of their petroleum assets by withdrawing their technical personnel. Petroleum production fell to near-zero levels. The British government froze Iranian government financial assets around the world and instituted an embargo on the purchase of Iranian oil. [49]

In 1953, after considerable economic turmoil for Iran, Shah Reza Pahlavi tried to dismiss Mossadeq as Prime Minister. There was violent public protest and the Shah left Iran, apparently having been deposed. But the U.S. and British governments, acting in collaboration with the military officers Mossadeq had dismissed, organized a coup d'état. Street mobs were hired to demonstrate against Mossadeq and then the military took control in the name of maintaining public order. The Shah returned to Iran and took control of the government. Mossadeq was tried and convicted of treason and sentenced to three years in prison and house arrest for the rest of his life. [49]

The details of US involvement in the 1953 coup were classified until recently. In June 2017, 64 years later, the US State Department released hundreds of previously classified documents described the operation, called Operation Ajax. [48]

Chapter 11. The White Revolution (June 1963) and approach to 1979 revolution

Populations have anti-government protests and demonstrations all the time. Sometimes the protests fizzle quickly. Sometimes the government acquiesces quickly, and makes the protests unnecessary. Sometimes the the protests lead to a "velvet revolution," where the government falls and is replaced with little or no bloodshed. At other times, the protests lead to full scale revolutions, with massacres, rapes, atrocities, mass slaughter, ethnic cleansing, and genocide.

Generational theory provides the tools for sorting out and explaining these different outcomes. With regard to question of whether a protest fizzles versus turning into a full-scale revolution, generational theory provides a clear answer. A full scale revolution, with massacres, rapes and atrocities, is so horrible that it traumatizes everyone who survives, and winners and losers alike vow never to let anything like it happen again. And they succeed, as long as they're alive, and they make sure that new protests and demonstrations by people in younger generations fizzle out as quickly as possible. But after 58-80 years, when most or all those survivors have retired or died, then there's nothing to inhibit the younger generations, and new protests can once again turn into full scale revolutions.

11.1. The White Revolution (June 1963) vs the Tobacco Revolt (1890)

In a previous chapter we described the Tobacco Revolt protests that occurred in 1890-92, and now we're going to describe the White Revolution protests that occurred in 1963. In both cases, older generations in the government suppressed the revolt, while the parents of the young protesters made sure that they didn't become violent. Thus, The Tobacco Revolt protests did not go any further because the state backed down at various stages, and the 1963 White Revolt protests did not spread further because the state was strong enough to suppress it quickly with an iron fist, and before the less daring crowds could have been encouraged to join the movement. [33]

However, in both cases the protests served the purpose of providing a dress rehearsal for the approaching full-scale bloody revolutions, in each case occurring about 15-16 years after the dress rehearsal protests. [33]

The White Revolution in 1963 was actually a government program instituted by the Shah. It included land reform, the nationalization of forests, the sale of state-owned enterprises to the private sector, a profit-sharing plan for industrial workers, and the formation of a Literacy Corps to eradicate illiteracy in rural areas. The White Revolution also granted Iranian women the right to vote, increased women's minimum legal marriage age to 18, and improved women's legal rights in divorce and child custody matters. [43]

These reforms were opposed by some of Iran's clergy, in particular Ayatollah Khomeini. Khomeini led the June 5, 1963 uprising, opposing the Shah and the White Revolution. In the course of this uprising, the authorities quelled resistance among the religious students in a seminary in the city of Qum, and a number of students lost their lives. Khomeini's activities eventually led to his exile to Iraq in 1964. [43]

It's well to remember the old saying that history doesn't repeat itself, but it rhymes. Protests following both the Tobacco Revolt and the White Revolution were 70 years apart, and they both fizzled fairly quickly, but they had a lot in common. They were both protests against government excesses. In both cases, the protests were were led by an élite group of citizens. The protests in the Tobacco Revolt were led by tobacco merchants who feared that their control of the tobacco marketplace and the bazaar in general was being usurped.

The protests following the White Revolution had the same effect but were led by a different set of élites. In this case, it was religious leaders who feared that they would lose their influence and control over sectors of society where they were preeminent. Things like land reform, improving literacy through better education, and granting women additional rights could all be viewed as threatening to the clerics and imams and their areas of traditional authority.

One particular member of Iran's clergy rose to prominence at this time: Ayatollah Ruhollah Khomeini, the cleric who later in 1979 was the leader of the bloody Great Islamic Revolution. On June 5, 1963, Khomeini led an uprising against the Shah's government that led to the deaths of a number of religious students. The Shah was able to crush the protests and exile to Khomeini to Iraq in 1964. [43]

11.2. Prelude to the 1979 Great Islamic Revolution

Shah Mohammad Reza Pahlavi's victory over Khomeini and the protesters gave him confidence to become increasingly autocratic The Shah saw himself as heir to the kings of ancient Iran, and in 1971 he held an extravagant celebration of 2,500 years of Persian monarchy. In 1976 he replaced the Islamic calendar with an "imperial" calendar, which began with the foundation of the Persian Empire more than 25 centuries earlier. These actions were viewed as anti-Islamic and resulted in religious opposition. [46]

The oil boom of the 1970s created enormous wealth for Iran, but the wealth was unequally distributed among the classes, leading to further discontent. In 1976, leading members of Khomeini's party, the National Front, published an open letter to the Shah, calling on his government to comply fully with the 1906 Constitution. In the Fall of 1977 the Iranian Writers' Association organized a series of poetry readings at the Goethe Institute in Tehran known as "Dah Shab" or Ten Nights. Towards the end of the ten nights, the writers and some students took to the streets, demanding an end to censorship. By the winter of 1978, major demonstrations became increasingly common in Iran's major cities. On January 16, 1979, Mohammad Reza Shah Pahlavi left Iran. On February 1, 1979, Ayatollah Ruhollah Khomeini returned from exile. [43]

The above narrative shows a clear trend during the 16-year period from the White Revolution of 1963 to the Islamic Revolution of 1979. At the beginning of that period, anti-government protests were weak and fizzled quickly. The frequency and potency of these protests increased gradually, and by the end of that period, the protests spread and became a bloody civil war.

From the point of view of generational theory, this trend is explained by the fact that in 1963, the generations of survivors of the bloody Constitutional Revolution were still in charge, and they were able to prevent small protests from growing into larger ones. During that 16-year period, those survivors gradually disappeared (retired or died), leaving behing younger generations with no personal memory of the horrors of the Constitutional Revolution and no fear of larger street protests. By 1979, there was no one left in charge to prevent a new bloody civil war.

Part IV. The Great Islamic Revolution (1979-present)

What happens in any civil war is that people who have lived to-gether on the same streets and villages for decades, where the wives have shared recipes and the kids have played together, suddenly turn on each other and start killing each other. In the 1994 Rwanda civil war, for example, a man in one tribe would pick up a machete, go next door and kill and dismember the man and children, rape the wife and then kill and dismember her. Many civil wars may not go to those extremes, but every civil war has some element of that.

Chapter 12. The rise of Ayatollah Ruhollah Khomeini

The leader of the insurgents in Iran's 1979 civil war was Ayatollah Ruhollah Khomeini, who had led the anti-government protests in the 1963 White Revolution, and ended up seeing hundreds of his follow-ers killed, after which he was sent into exile by Mohammad Reza Shah Pahlavi. When Khomeini made his triumphant return from 16 years of exile to Tehran on February 1, 1979, he was ready for revenge.

Khomeini had already gotten his revenge on the Shah. Although he had been in exile, he was able in 1978-79 to incite widespread anti-Shah uprisings based on discontent with a populist ideology tied to Islamic principles and calls for the overthrow of the Shah. The upris-ings forced the Shah's government to collapse and, suffering from cancer, the Shah went into exile and left Iran on January 16, 1979. He lived in Egypt, Morocco, the Bahamas, and Mexico before going to the United States for treatment of lymphatic cancer, where he died. [47]

Thousands of people were killed in Iran's civil war, including thousands who were jailed or executed by Khomeini. Khomeini claims that 60,000 people were killed. Here's a paragraph from Khomeini's 1979 constitution:

> "After slightly more than a year of continuous and unrelent-ing struggle, the sapling of the Revolution, watered by the blood of more than 60,000 martyrs and 100,000 wounded and

disabled, not to mention billions of tumans' worth of property damage, came to bear fruit amidst the cries of "Independence! Freedom! Islamic government!" This great movement, which attained victory through reliance upon faith, unity, and the decisiveness of its leadership at every critical and sensitive juncture, as well as the self-sacrificing spirit of the people, succeeded in upsetting all the calculations of imperialism and destroying all its connections and institutions, thereby opening a new chapter in the history of all embracing popular revolutions of the world." [34]

However, analysts outside of Iran question the 60,000 figure, and give much lower estimates of 3,000-4,000.

Chapter 13. The 'causes' of the Great Islamic Revolution

A civil war in which people slaughter, rape and torture other people who had formerly been their friends and neighbors creates an outcome which is vastly different from other types of war (i.e., external wars, where the two sides live in different countries or regions, and one side invades the other).

Such a civil war has to be settled, as one side forces the other side into submission. But people on both sides, winners and losers, are traumatized by the atrocities that they had committed on their friends and neighbors, and the atrocities that their friends and neighbors had committed on them. There is no way for a society to return to "normal life" after such a civil war ends. And it's important to emphasize this: People are traumatized by their own atrocities as much as, and probably more than, the atrocities that others committed on them.

So after any such war ends, there are two particular societal changes that become apparent as the decades pass:

- The survivors of the civil war are so traumatized that they literally devote their lives to making sure that it doesn't happen again, and are even willing to swallow compromises that they dislike, since nothing is worse than going through another civil war. That's why the 1963 White Revolution protests fizzled — there were survivors of the Constitutional Revolution still alive and still sufficiently in control of younger generations that they could still make sure that the White Revolution protests fizzled.

- The younger generations, people who grew up after the Constitutional Revolution, did not suffer the trauma of seeing their side and the other side commit atrocities. Instead, all they know about what happened is the atrocities committed by the other side, filtered by their parents' war stories that carefully omit anything about their own atrocities. When younger generations hear about atrocities committed by their own side, they reject them as "fake news." So when their parents, the survivors of the preceding civil war, finally die off, all they're left with is a highly filtered story of what happened, and an overwhelming desire for revenge. That's the "cause" of the 1979 revolution.

These generational principles apply to any civil war. History doesn't repeat itself, but it rhymes. The Tobacco Revolt led 15 years later to the Constitutional Revolution, which was a civil war that began with an insurgency led by students, merchants and shopkeepers, and spread to the rest of the population. The White Revolution led 16 years later to the Islamic Revolution, which was a civil war that began with an insurgency led by students and clerics, and spread to the rest of the population.

That's the "cause" of the Great Islamic Revolution. In one way or another, it had to occur in order for younger generations to exact revenge for the atrocities committed during the Constitutional Revolution. This revenge may be exacted in different possible ways, but it will be exacted in one way or another.

Chapter 14. The excuses for the Great Islamic Revolution

So now we'll turn to what historians say are the "causes" of the 1979 civil war. They are "causes" only to the extent that they explain the manner in which the revenge was exacted, and what excuses are given for the new atrocities that will occur.

This is important. If Khomeini, or any other civil war leader, is going to direct his followers to commit slaughter, rapes, arrests, torture and other atrocities, then he has to provide his followers with excuses and justifications that go beyond "well, I just want to get even for what happened to my great-grandmother." Even though they're just excuses, the leaders uses them to motivate his followers to kill. Then, after the war ends, they provide justifications for why the war occurred at all, and they provide historians with a way to analyze the war in the context of their own ideologies.

- Many historians list American interference in Iran as a principal cause, starting with the CIA coup in 1953. There are two major problems with this explanation. First, it doesn't explain why there was a 26 year delay from 1953 to the 1979 revolution. And second, Iran has experienced foreign intervention from Britain and Russia at least since the early 1800s. In fact, foreign intervention in Iran was pretty much continuous. Historians would have to explain why continuous foreign intervention suddenly became so important in 1979 as to cause a revolution.

  But historians are correct that American intervention played a major role in the excuses and justifications for the 1979 revolution, and has been a major factor in Iran's domestic policies ever since, starting with the Iranian Hostage Crisis of 1979-81.

- There were various economic factors given as causes of the 1979 revolution. Although petroleum revenues continued to be a major source of income for Iran in the 1970s, world monetary instability and fluctuations in Western oil consumption seriously threatened the country's economy, which had been rapidly expanding since the early 1950s and was still directed in large part toward high-cost projects and programs. A decade of extraordinary economic growth, heavy government spending, and a boom in oil prices led to high rates of inflation and the stagnation of Iranians' buying power and standard of living. [4]

It's very hard to support the view that economic conditions caused a revolution, since economic ups and downs occur all the time. However, it is possible that a severe economic recession, which happened in the late 1970s in Iran, is the TRIGGER of a revolution, as opposed to its cause. This means that the revolution was going to occur anyway, but it might have occurred a little earlier or a little later, depending on the economic conditions.

- Another reason usually given as a cause was the increasing repression by the regime of Mohammad Reza Shah Pahlavi in the 1970s. Outlets for political participation were minimal, and opposition parties such as Khomeini's National Front (a loose coalition of nationalists, clerics, and noncommunist left-wing parties) and the pro-Soviet Tudeh ("Masses") Party were marginalized or outlawed. Social and political protest was often met with censorship, surveillance, or harassment, and illegal detention and torture were common. [4]

This is a very interesting reason, because it's similar to reasons given for the Constitutional Revolution, and the reason why the insurgents in 1905 were demanding a written constitution, to control the excesses of the leaders. However, it's not a cause, so much as a coincident condition. What this means is that popular unrest increases, the regime becomes increasingly repressive, which causes further unrest, leading to a vicious cycle. The reason why social unrest is increasing in the first place is because the survivors of the Constitutional Revolution were quickly dying off, and the young people are no longer being controlled by their conservative parents.

- Another theory claims that the cause of the 1979 revolution was the ideology developed by Khomeini in the early 1970s. It argues that the 1963 White Revolution fizzled because this ideology was not then available, as it was in 1979. The ideology referred to is the ancient Shia doctrine of Guardianship of the Jurist, which Khomeini reinterpreted in such as way as to make himself almost an absolute dictator, guided by his personal interpretation of Shia Islamic law. The irony is that he used this doctrine to replace the nearly absolute dictatorship of the Shah with the nearly absolute dictatorship of himself,

47

claiming that he was different because he was guided by Shia Islamic law, while the Shah was not. [9]

As we've previously described, the reason that the 1963 White Revolution fizzled was because the survivors of the 1905 Constitutional Revolution were still around to suppress the excesses of their children, while they were gone by 1979.

But the Guardianship of the Jurist was an extremely important element of Khomeini's 1979 revolution. As we've said before, when a leader wants to convince his followers to torture, rape and kill political opponents, then he has to give his followers a reason. In the case of a religious war, such as Catholics against Protestants or Christians against Jews or Hindus against Muslims, the easiest justification is religious — the other side are infidels who are going to hell anyway so there's no harm in torturing and killing them.

But Khomeini's civil war was not a directly religious war, since the people on both sides were Shia Muslims. Khomeini needed it to be a religious war, since he needed a religious justification to justify telling his followers to kill, torture and commit atrocities, and so his reinterpretation of the ancient Shia doctrine of Guardianship of the Jurist served this purpose well. Guardianship of the Jurist remains today as the most important core concept guiding the Iran's current government, and so we'll be discussing it at length in a later chapter.

A civil war is not like an external war, where an army from one country invades another country. In a civil war, we're talking about people who live in the same villages, or even the same streets, where the wives had shared recipes and the children had played with each other.

When we talk about the "causes" of any civil war, then we have to provide an explanation of why a man would pick up a weapon, go next door, kill the husband and children, rape the wife, and dismember all of them. No man would be motivated to do this by a CIA coup that occurred 26 years earlier. No man would do this because he didn't have enough money. This kind of action can only be explained by long-held desires for revenge, combined with the removal of inhibiting factors, particularly the man's parents.

Chapter 15. Khomeini's great massacre of 1988

Ayatollah Khomeini's bloodthirsty lusts reached a kind of peak in 1988 when he ordered the massacre of tens of thousands of political prisoners and political enemies, especially those in the People's Mojahedin Organization of Iran (PMOI or MEK). He issued this decree in July 1988:

> "Whoever at any stage continues to belong to the PMOI must be executed. Annihilate the enemies of Islam immediately! ...Those who are in prisons throughout the country and remain steadfast in their support for PMOI are waging war on God and are condemned to execution...It is naïve to show mercy to those who wage war on God." [6]

Apparently the form of torture that excited Khomeini the most was bastinado, beating the soles of someone's feet. Khomeini must have liked it because it inflicts maximum pain while leaving no visible scars.

In 2001 Grand Ayatollah Hossein Ali Montazeri, former designated successor to Khomeini, published a memoir which contains details of the 1988 massacre. Iran had killed a large number of political prisoners throughout the 1980s, so why the sudden increase in 1988? The witnesses' testimonies suggest that the regime was worried about the large number of unrepentant political prisoners due to be released after the end of the Iran/Iraq war, and so decided to purge its prisons of troublesome elements once and for all. [5]

Many of the people whom Khomeini killed had been in prison for years as political prisoners. They were hung from cranes, four at a time, or in groups of six from ropes hanging from the front of the stage in an assembly hall; some were taken to army barracks at night, directed to make their wills and then shot by firing squad. Their bodies were doused with disinfectant, packed in refrigerated trucks and buried by night in mass graves. Months later their families, desperate for information about their children or their partners, would be handed a plastic bag with their few possessions. They would be refused any information about the location of the graves and ordered never to mourn them in public. By mid-August 1988, thousands of prisoners had been killed in this manner by the state – without trial, without appeal and utterly without mercy. [7]

Ayatollah Hossein-Ali Montazeri, a cleric who had for ten years been the designated successor to Supreme Leader Ayatollah Khomeini, strongly protested against the mass executions and called for a moratorium, but Khomeini insisted that there should be no mercy shown and ordered that all prisoners, including even teenagers and pregnant women, be put to death immediately. Montazeri then fell out of favor, and was no longer considered a successor to Khomeini. [6]

This shows the power of a civil war leader using a religious justification to kill, rape, torture people on the other side, especially innocent women and children. Even after the war, the religious justification continues for further atrocities, almost like a James Bond 007 "license to kill, arrest, rape, and torture" with impunity. On my web site, I've documented this same sort of "license to kill, arrest, rape, and torture" in a number of countries in a number of countries following a religious or ethnic civil war, including Democratic Republic of Congo, Zimbabwe, Cameroon, Uganda, Rwanda, Burundi and, outside of Africa, Syria, Burma (Myanmar), South Korea, China, Vietnam and Cambodia.

Many of today's leaders in Iran fully supported and participated in the 1988 massacre. The new so-called "moderate" President of Iran, Hassan Rouhani, was Deputy Commander-in-chief of the regime's armed forces at the time of the massacres and, since 1982, was a member of regime's Supreme Defence Council, so was fully aware of the crime and in full conformity with it. [6]

Chapter 16. Iranian hostage crisis

The Iran hostage crisis was tangential to the Iranian civil war, but it has been responsible for the enormous dislike that Americans feel towards Iran since then. And those Iranians who participated in the hostage crisis would undoubtedly say that it was caused by the 1953 CIA coup. So there's a lesson to be learned from how a single act can have repercussions that last for decades.

In July 1979, Ayatollah Ruhollah Khomeini's supporters forced Mohammad Reza Shah Pahlavi to flee Iran and flee to Egypt. Pahlavi had already been diagnosed with cancer, and in October 1979 President Jimmy Carter, as a humanitarian act, allowed Pahlavi to enter the U.S. for treatment of an advanced malignant lymphoma. This act infuriated a group of students in Tehran, who scaled the walls of the American embassy and seized 66 hostages. Some hostages were released, but by summer 1980, 52 hostages remained. [8]

The disaster was compounded in April 1980, when a US military operation attempting to rescue the hostages failed spectacularly, killing eight soldiers when a helicopter crashed into a transport plane. [8]

The Iranian hostage crisis ran for 444 days, from November 4, 1979, to January 21, 1981, the day of Ronald Reagan's inauguration.

Five years after that, an Iranian girl asked me why Americans hated Iranians so much. I told her that every day for over a year, news anchor Walter Cronkite would begin his daily newscast saying something like, "Good evening from CBS News, on day 276 of the Iranian hostage crisis." Hearing that made her cry.

Part V. Pre-Islamic Persian empires

Chapter 17. The cycles of history

Persia's civilization is one of the longest and proudest in the world, and the ancient Persian empires are some of the greatest in the history of the world.

The people of Iran today are well aware of their proud history, and a desire to restore some of these ancient days of glory is part of the motivation for many of their decisions. However, like many other things, these empires were cyclical, alternating between success and collapse.

There are many kinds of cycles in history, and many of them are based on the following general concept: If a group or society or nation becomes successful, and remains successful for a long time, then they begin to count on success as inevitable, and they take risks and incur debts. The greater the success, and the longer the success lasts, then the risks and the debts become greater and greater. As soon as any setback occurs, even a small setback, then suddenly the risks become unsustainable and the debts cannot be repaid, resulting in a total collapse. Once the society recovers from the collapse, it rebuilds itself and becomes successful again, and the cycle repeats.

In other words, success causes collapse, and collapse causes success.

In the area of finance, the relevant concept is "Minsky Moment," named after economist Hyman Minsky. When a stock market is bullish for a long time, then it experiences highly inflated market speculation and unsustainable growth. Eventually a recession or other financial setback leads to a crisis known as a "Minsky Moment." The longer the bull market was, the bigger the crisis, to the extent of being a complete stock market crash. [52]

Prominent historians such as Oswald Spengler (1880–1936) and Arnold Toynbee (1889–1975) have identified major civilization cycles throughout history, and presented theories to explain them. Spengler proposed that individual societies have a life cycle similar to living organisms: they experience periods of growth, maturity, and decline. According to him, these cycles repeat themselves as new societies develop. Toynbee was influenced by his reading of Spengler's work. He argued that civilizations emerge when faced with physical or social challenges. He believed that the history of a civilization was largely the record of its response to a unique challenge. On a larger scale, he saw that history moved through periods governed by universal states followed by shorter periods of religious rule. In Toynbee's view, societies decline when they fail to surmount a challenge and thereafter lose social cohesiveness. However, he acknowledged the possibility that a civilization could repeatedly meet its challenges. Fernand Braudel (1902–1985) expanded these theories by developing a system that encompassed short-term (individual), medium-term (social), and long-term (geographical) time periods. [53]

Starting from ancient times, communities pass from a crude and barbaric beginning, marked by unruly courage and fierce clan solidarity, to a dynamic and well-ordered society, poised to wield power, explore natural and human resources, acquire wealth, enjoy leisure, and develop arts and crafts, giving birth in the process to a distinct culture. The culture thus created develops as long as the community possesses its inner strength and creative power. It has to maintain and safeguard itself against external enemies and internal dissent and subversion. The comfort, leisure, and luxury, and, more importantly, the sheer weight of time that corrodes and enfeebles every dynasty, social order, and culture, eventually sap the energy and exhaust the cultural potentials of the community. Personal concerns take precedence over public ones; corruption becomes rampant, and stagnation sets in. The very struggle to uphold the viability of a given culture over a long stretch of time consumes in the end its inner resources, and the culture begins to decline. The society can no longer defend itself against claimants from within or without, poised to establish a new ruling power and possibly start a new culture. Finally the community becomes subservient to a new, rising culture and drifts along as its cultural or political client. [51]

These kinds of cycles prevailed in the histories of ancient Persia, according to analyses by Iranian scholars. They view the total defeat of Elam and the sack of Susa by Assurbanipal in 639 BC, the capture of Babylon by Cyrus in 539 BC, the conquest of Egypt by Cambyses in 525 BC, the fall of Rome at the hand of Germanic invaders in 476 AD, and the Arab conquest of Sasanian Persia in the 7th century AD as representing the outcome of cultural fatigue induced by old age. Modern Persians and Greeks hardly show the same creative energy and possess the same moral fiber that characterized them in the heydays of their ancestral civilizations. The geography had not changed, but the peoples had: they had aged. Individual dynasties follow the same trajectory, except that often their decline and fall does not presage the end of a culture, only their own rule. The fall of the Achaem-enids in 330 BC, of the Ummayads in 750 AD, of the Persian branch of the Ghaznavids in 1186, of the Tudors in 1603, or the extinction of the Bourbon pretenders to the throne of France in 1883, did not toll the bells signaling the end of their respective cultures. [51]

Chapter 18. Summary of pre-Islamic Persian empires

In the following chapters, we'll describe the major Persian empires. Here's a summary:

- The Elamite Dynasties (2800 BC - 550 BC) and the Median Empire (728 - 550 BC) were early tribal empires whose culture influenced the Persians for centuries to come. Some historians believe that today's Kurds are the descendants of the Medes, though this is disputed by others.

- The Magi were not a empire, but they were "keepers of the faith," a tribe of clerics, possibly including Zoroaster (Zarathustra), that developed and protected the Zoroastrianism religion. The three wise men that brought gifts to Jesus in the manger were Magis.

- King Cyrus the Great (580-529 BC) is the great hero of Persia's antiquity. Cyrus is considered to be the founder of Iran, because he conquered and united the Medes and all the Persian tribes.

- The Achaemenid Empire (550 - 331 BC) was King Cyrus's empire, which was the greatest empire the world had seen to that time.

- Alexander the Great (356-323 BC) is the "anti-Cyrus," the great villain of Persia's antiquity. He conquered and destroyed the Achaemenid Empire, and particularly sacked and leveled its capital city, Persepolis, destroying centuries of Persian culture and art, as well as Zoroastrian temples and sacred texts.

- The Seleucid Empire (323-150 BC) is named after Alexander's general Seleucus, who took control of Iran after Alexander's death. This is called the Hellenistic period of Persia, because of the widespread adoption of Greek culture and art.

- The Parthian Empire (247 BC-226 AD) broke off from the Seleucids after the invasion by the Arsacids, and became the anti-Greek empire, reviving the traditional Iranian culture.

- The Roman-Parthian Wars (53 BC - 217 AD) began in 53 BC with a disastrous defeat for the Romans by the Persians, followed by centuries of failed attempts by Rome to subjugate

Parthia. By 100 BC, there were two major empires in the region, Rome and Parthia, and a diplomatic agreement in 93 BC succeeded only temporarily.

- The Sassanid Empire (226 - 651 AD) was the last Persian empire before the conquest by Islamic Arabs in 651. It is considered by the Iranian people to be a highlight of their civilization, since it was the first Persian empire since conquest by Alexander the Great that felt truly "Iranian."

Chapter 19. Persian history — early dynasties

It is not my intention to provide a king-by-king or battle-by-battle history of ancient Persia, for several reasons. First, and most obviously, that kind of history is too large and complex for a book like this. Second, those details are all available on the internet for anyone interested. Indeed, the references and links we provide in this exposition will give almost anyone more detailed information than they want.

The third reason is that these details are completely unknown to most Iranians today, even people with knowledge of Iranian history, and so are irrelevant for our purposes. We will try to focus on those individuals (such as Zoroaster or Cyrus the Great) and those events (such as the rise of the Achaemenid, Seleucid, Parthian, and Sassanid empires) that knowledgeable Iranians think of with pride, and so affect day to day decisions in lives and politics.

Generational theory analyzes behaviors and actions taken by entire populations or generations, and so we focus on the historical people and events that will affect the behavior and actions of entire populations and generations.

Elamite Dynasties (2800 BC - 550 BC). The beginnings of the Elam culture existed from at least 3500 BC, and existing Elamite pottery shows an advanced stage of geometrical designs and stylized human and animal forms. A major military conquest in 2004 BC brought the Elamite dynasty centered in Anshan a period of prosperity in many ways on a par with Babylonian and Assyrian civilizations and a worthy rival to them. Elam repeatedly challenged Assyrian power, but eventually in 639 BC the cycle ended, when the Assyrians conquered Elam, destroyed most of its cities, and assimilated the people into the Assyrian Empire. By 550 BC and the conquest by Cyrus the Great, it had disappeared and never rose again as an independent power. [51] [54]

Median Empire (728 - 550 BC) Of the numerous Iranian tribes who had settled in Iranian plateau, it was the Medes tribe that grew in power and achieved prominence. In 612 BC, Median leader Cyaxares, in alliance with the Babylonians, attacked the Assyrian capital, Nineveh. Their combined forces succeeded in bringing the Assyrian Empire down, thus eliminating a power that had ruled with ruthless efficiency over the Middle East for several centuries. The Assyrian domain was divided between the Medes and the Babylonians. [51]

The formation of the powerful Median kingdom stretching from northern Mesopotamia to Bactria, finally defeated by Cyrus the Great in 550 BC, is one of the turning points of Iranian history. However, the rise and fall of the Median kingdom, like that of the Achaemenid Empire to come, conforms to the classic pattern of a dynamic people rising from tribal beginnings to a position of immense monarchical power before declining and ceding power to a younger force. [51]

The Magi - Zoroaster (Zarathustra) and Zoroastrianism. The existence of an actual person named Zoroaster (Greek name) or Zarathustra (Persian name) is still questioned by some scholars, but the importance of the religion Zoroastrianism as an influential religion is unquestioned. The date of Zoroaster's birth is sometimes given as around 660 BC, with his death occurring around the time of the conquest by Cyrus the Great. Others claim that Zoroaster lived as much as 1000 years earlier. [26]

Whether and when Zoroaster actually lived, the perception today is that Zoroaster developed Zoroastrianism, with concepts that have influenced all religions since then. One concept is monotheism — one god, whom he referred to as Ahura Mazda, or the "Wise Lord." Just as important was the concept of dualism, according to which history is a cosmic struggle between the powers of good, i.e., light versus evil or darkness. Every religion since then has been forced to deal with these two concepts, because they present an important conflict: If there's only one god, the creator, but there is both good and evil in the universe, then it follows that the creator created evil as well as good. Every religion must then answer the question of how it's possible that a benevolent creator god was responsible for creating evil. [26] [29]

Early forms of Zoroastrianism were around for centuries, but the religion only became influential when it was adopted by the Magi, a hereditary clan of priests that is believed to have been one of the Median tribes. The popularity of Zoroastrianism waned under Alexander the Great, but surged again in the Parthian and Sassanid empires. Zoroastrianism remained a powerful religious force in Persia until the conquest by the Muslim Arabs in 651. Today, Zoroastrianism still has many followers, although its practice is frowned upon by Iran's hardline government. [30]

In 2016, when the vitriolic war of words between Iran and Saudi Arabia appeared to be leading to a military confrontation, Iran's Supreme Leader Ayatollah Seyed Ali Khamenei said, "Saudi rulers ... are disgraced and misguided people who think their survival ... is dependent on defending the arrogant powers of the world, on alliances with Zionism and the U.S. and on fulfilling their demands." [103]

Saudi Arabia's leading cleric Grand Mufti Sheikh Abdulaziz Al al-Sheik responded: "We must understand that these [Iranians] are not Muslims, they are the sons of the Magi, and their hostility to Muslims is old and specifically with the Sunnis and the community." So the Saudi cleric made a very serious accusation — that the Iranians were Zoroastrians, and that Zoroastrians are not Muslims. [103]

Chapter 20. Cyrus the Great and the Achaemenid Persian empire (550-331 BC)

Iranians take great pride that the Achaemenid Persian empire, founded by Cyrus the Great, was the largest that the ancient world had seen, extending from Anatolia and Egypt across western Asia to northern India and Central Asia. [36]

King Cyrus the Great (580-529 BC) is considered to be the founder of Iran because he conquered and united the Medes and all the Persian tribes into a single Achaemenid empire, which was the greatest empire the world had seen to that time.

Around 550 BC, western Asia was divided into three kingdoms: the Babylonian empire, the Median empire, and Lydia. Cyrus, Prince of Anzan in Elam, conquered them in turn. He conquered the Median Empire in 550 BC and became the King of Media. In 546 BC, he defeated Lydia, and annexed Asia Minor to his realm. In 539, he marched against Babylon. In 538 BC, Babylon surrendered, and Cyrus allowed the Jews to return to Palestine. [25]

In March 2018, Israel's prime minister Benjamin Netanyahu visited the White House, and he made remarks crediting Cyrus the Great with liberating the Jews from the Babylonians, and allowing them to return to the promised land in Palestine:

> "I want to tell you that the Jewish people have a long memory, so we remember the proclamation of the great king, Cyrus the Great, the Persian king 2,500 years ago. He proclaimed that the Jewish exiles in Babylon could come back and rebuild our Temple in Jerusalem. We remember a hundred years ago, Lord Balfour, who issued the Balfour Proclamation that recognized the rights of the Jewish people in our ancestral homeland. We remember 70 years ago, President Harry S. Truman was the first leader to recognize the Jewish state. And we remember how a few weeks ago, President Donald J. Trump recognized Jerusalem as Israel's capital. Mr. President, this will be remembered by our people through the ages." [55]

Cyrus was killed in battle in 529 or 530 BC.

Ruins of Palace at Darius in Persepolis, destroyed by Alexander the Great

A few years after Cyrus' death, Darius the Great emerged as king, ruling from 522 BC until his death in 486 BC. While Cyrus was the conqueror, Darius was the administrator. Under Darius the empire was stabilized, with roads for communication and a system of governors (satraps) established. He added northwestern India to the Achaemenid realm and initiated two major building projects: the construction of royal buildings at Susa and the creation of the new dynastic center of Persepolis, the buildings of which were decorated by Darius and his successors with stone reliefs and carvings. These show tributaries from different parts of the empire processing toward the enthroned king or conveying the king's throne. The impression is of a harmonious empire supported by its numerous peoples. Darius also consolidated Persia's western conquests in the Aegean. [36]

The next king of the Achaemenid Empire is best known for an enormous blunder that he committed during his expeditionary invasion of Greece in 480 BC.

Xerxes I (ruled 486-465 BCE), also called Xerxes the Great became King of the Achaemenid Empire on the death of Darius. He launched an invasion of Greece that turned out to be a huge disaster for Xerxes and the Persians. Xerxes' blunder was ordering the burning of the Acropolis in Athens. This happened in 480 BC, and Alexander the Great got revenge a century and a half later, in 331 BC, when he ordered the destruction of Persepolis, the capital city of the Achaemenid Empire.

The Achaemenid Empire survived for another 150 years, and much of that time was spent in wars with the Greek states in the western part of the empire. Those wars continued sporadically until one particular Greek, Alexander the Great of Macedon, conquered the Persian empire in 330 BC.

Chapter 21. Alexander the Great and the Seleucid Empire (323-150 BC)

When Alexander the Great of Macedon conquered Persia in 330 BC, it was the end of the "truly Iranian" civilization for centuries, until the rise of the Sassanian Empire in 226 AD.

Most of what we know about Alexander's invasion of Achaemenid — indeed, most of what we know about all of the Achaemenid empire — is from Greek sources, and so much of this information is biased, and leans toward gloating about Greek victories. The story of Alexander's sacking of Persopolis in 331 BC was told three centuries later by the Greek historian Diodorus of Sicily:

"Alexander held games in honor of his victories. He performed costly sacrifices to the gods and entertained his friends bountifully. While they were feasting and the drinking was far advanced, as they began to be drunken, a madness took possession of the minds of the intoxicated guests. At this point one of the women present, Thais by name and Athenian by origin, said that for Alexander it would be the finest of all his feats in Asia if he joined them in a triumphal procession, set fire to the palaces, and permitted women's hands in a minute to extinguish the famed accomplishments of the Persians. This was said to men who were still young and giddy with wine, and so, as would be expected, someone shouted out to form up and to light torches, and urged all to take vengeance for the destruction of the Greek temples [burned by the Persians when they invaded Athens in 480 BCE]. Others took up the cry and said that this was a deed worthy of Alexander alone. When the king had caught fire at their words, all leaped up from their couches and passed the word along to form a victory procession in honor of the god Dionysus. Promptly many torches were gathered. Female musicians were present at the banquet, so the king led them all out to the sound of voices and flutes and pipes, Thais the courtesan leading the whole performance. She was the first, after the king, to hurl her blazing torch into the palace. As the others all did the same, immediately the entire palace area was consumed, so great was the conflagration. It was most remarkable that the impious act of Xerxes, king of the Persians, against the Acropolis at Athens should have been repaid in kind after many years by one woman, a citizen of the land which had suffered it, and in sport." [58]

So the sequence of events was that Achaemenid King Xerxes invaded Greece and burned the Acropolis in 480 BC, and then Greek military leader Alexander the Great invaded the Achaemenid Empire and burned Persepolis in 331 BC. Western history books portray this as a great achievement by Alexander the Great, perhaps the greatest military genius of all time, supposedly in a crusade to bring civilization and culture to the barbaric East. But the Persians, including the Iranians today, look at it far differently. [59]

In the Persian view, not only did Alexander raze Persepolis to the ground following a night of drunken excess, he also encouraged the destruction of cultural and religious sites throughout the empire. In particular, the destruction of the Zoroastrian temples and holy scriptures was a calamity for the Magi, the Zoroastrian priesthood. [59]

When Alexander died at age 33 in 323 BC, his enormous empire was split up into about a dozen pieces among his generals. The eastern portion of Alexander's conquered lands from Syria to Central Asia, including the lands inhabited by the Iranians, came under the rule of Seleucus. [51]

The death of Alexander in 323 BC led to a series of successor wars among Alexander's generals, competing for different pieces of the empire. The Greek general Seleucus I Nicator (358-281 BC), was an active participant in those wars, competing with the likes of Perdiccos, Ptolemy, and Antigonos for different pieces. [56]

Seleucus's name was given to the Seleucid Empire, which continued to expand for about 100 years under its successors, until it was forced to retreat from the Arsacids. At the height of its power, the Seleucid Empire included central Anatolia, the Levant, Mesopotamia, Persia, today's Turkmenistan, Pamir and parts of Pakistan. [27]

The most important legacy of Alexander's military and political triumphs, however, lay in the cultural field. With him and his successors the Greek civilization spread in the entire Achaemenid domain, which adopted Greek institutions and religious views. The adoption of several aspects of Greek civilization, such as the widespread use of coinage, the system of weights and measures (derham and dinar in Persian symbolize their legacy in this respect), building techniques, and the legend "Philhellene" (admirer of the Greeks) appearing on Arsacid coins represented a process of Westernization that began with the Seleucids and continued into the Arsacid times. The fact that in

Persian the names of most precious stones and jewels, such as dia-
mond, ruby, emerald, silver (sim), agate, and possibly pearl, are derived from Greek, is itself an indication of the wealth and luxury of
the Greek and Macedonian ruling classes in Iran. The Iranian elite,
eager to save their skin and retain their privileges, were the first to
adapt themselves to Greek ways. [51]

However, one group of Persian elite were definitely not impressed
with the Greek culture. The Magis and Zoroastrian clergy remained
adamant in their defiance of Alexander. They dubbed him "Alexander
the cursed" and saw in him the destroyer of Iranian empire, of Zoroastrian temples, and the one responsible for the burning of their holy
scriptures. In the countryside people were naturally far less affected
by the Greek foreign culture, and continued with their own religious
beliefs, practices, and superstitions. [51]

Chapter 22. The Arsacids and the Parthian Empire (247 BC-226 AD).

22.1. Arsaces I conquest of Parthia (247 BC)

In 247 BC, Arsaces I of Parthia, leader of the Parni tribe, conquered the Parthia region in Iran's northeast, then a satrapy (province) in rebellion against the Seleucid Empire. The Parthian Empire, also known as the Arsacid Empire, was a major Iranian political and cultural power in ancient Persia. At its height, the Parthian Empire stretched from the northern reaches of the Euphrates, in what is now south-eastern Turkey, to eastern Iran. The empire, located on the Silk Road trade route between the Roman Empire in the Mediterranean Basin and Han Empire of China, became a center of trade and commerce. [27]

The Parthians largely adopted the art, architecture, religious beliefs, and royal insignia of their culturally heterogeneous empire, which encompassed Persian, Hellenistic, and regional cultures. For about the first half of its existence, the Arsacid court adopted elements of Greek culture, though it eventually saw a gradual revival of Iranian traditions. [27]

For the rest of its existence, the Parthians were fighting multiple wars on its boundaries, with some losses and some victories. However, it's the wars with the Roman Empire that determined its fate.

22.2. Roman-Parthian Wars (53 BC - 217 AD)

By the beginning of the first century BC, there were two major empires in the region, the Roman Empire and the Parthian Empire. In fact, most of what is known about the Parthian Empire today comes from Roman sources. [28]

There was a major diplomatic event at the time. In 92 BC, the Romans and the Parthians made an agreement that the Euphrates River would serve as the border between Parthia and Rome. [27] [57]

The Roman-Parthian Wars were a series of cultural clashes between the eastern and western titans of the ancient world. Parthia was the antithesis of Rome, in culture, in politics, and on the battlefield. What started out as a diplomatic meeting between leaders of the two kingdoms in 92 BCE eventually led to a string of wars, starting with the Battle of Carrhae in 53 BC and ending with the Battle of Nisibis in 217 AD. [28]

The Battle of Carrhae (53 BC) is well known because the outcome was such a major shock to both the Romans and the Parthians. Crassus, a millionaire politician, also wished to establish himself as a general of the stature of his triumviral colleagues, Pompey and Caesar. He chose to establish himself as a great general by invading Parthia, where he was a poor general and an ineffective commander. The result of this attempt to establish Crassus' military prestige led to some 20,000 Roman deaths, with another 10,000 captured. Perceptions changed, and Parthia had emerged as a great power able to crush Roman legions at will. [57]

At the time of Crassus's disastrous invasion of Parthia, the King of Parthia was Orodes II. According to one history, Orodes was sitting alongside the Armenian king Artavasdes II, and the two were watching a performance of The Bacchae by the Greek playwright Euripides (c. 480-406 BC), when the head of Crassus was brought to the Orodes at the theatre. The producer of the play decided to use Crassus' actual severed head in place of the stage-prop head of Pentheus. [27]

While they still held a considerable amount of land, Parthia's empire was initially not as large as the Seleucid empire, though they gradually conquered the latter's territory. In the end, the Parthians ruled from the borders of India to the frontiers of Armenia, and from fringes of Central Asia to the Indian Ocean. Rome, the other massive empire of the time, stretched from Northern Europe to North Africa, from the Atlantic Ocean to the Near East, and would eventually adjoin Parthia. [28]

The Parthians managed to defend their territory and stay in power for over 500 years (247 BC - 224 AD), the longest a dynasty has ruled in Iran, even though inevitable signs of weakness and exhaustion were noticeable towards the end of their rule.

Chapter 23. The Sassanid Empire (226-651 AD)

Many Iranians today consider the Achaemenid and Sassanid empires to be the heights of Iranian civilization and culture, separated by a Hellenized (Greek) period with the Selucids and Parthians, and then followed by an Islamic period after the Sassanids.

Just as the Parthians had conquered all the Seleucid territories by 155 BC, the Parthians themselves fell to Ardeshir I, who was a Persian for he came from the province of Fars (originally known as Pars, which is where the word Persian comes from) from where the Achaemenids came. He installed the Sassanid dynasty under the family name of his forefather Sasan. [60]

The Sassanians then started a process that would reinstate the values of Iranian culture. Although certainly still Hellenized, the Sassanians started a process of "Iranization" unlike the Parthians before them: Zoroastrianism became one of the founding stones of the Empire — though religious minorities such as Jews, Christians, Manicheans, and other faiths of the Iranian people would play an important part. Some of the Sassanian kings even married Jewish and Christian women. [60]

For 400 years the Sassanian Empire was the major power in the Near East as the rival of the Late Roman Empire. Not only that, but they sustained relations with the Tang Dynasty of China and several Indian Kingdoms where their products and culture were held in high esteem. [60]

Part VI. Persian history after the conquest by Islamic Arabs

Chapter 24. The fall of the Sassanian Empire to the Islamic Arabs (630-651)

In the end, the Sassanians did not fall to the Romans, but instead fell to the Arabs.

24.1. The war between the Sassanians and the Byzantines

By 600 AD, the Roman Empire had fallen, and its successor was the Eastern Roman Empire, the Greek Byzantine Empire, with its capital in the city of Byzantium, later called Constantinople, later called Istanbul. So there were two great empires in the Near East: the Byzantines (330?–1453 AD) and the Sassanians (224–651 AD). [61]

Just as there had been frequent border wars between the Parthians and the Romans, there were frequent border wars between the Sassanids and the Byzantines. What is sometimes called "the last great war of antiquity" was the war between the Byzantine Empire and the Sassanid Empire, 603-628 AD. The Sassanids were winning the war, and were on the verge of re-establishing the boundaries of the Achaemenid Empire (559-330 BC).

Unexpectedly, the tides turned, leading to what has been called "one of the most astonishing reversals of fortune in the annals of war." Suddenly, the Sassanians lost to the Byzantines. But that wasn't all. [61]

The Sassanian empire in the early 7th century was ruled by a religion-backed centralized monarchy with an elaborate bureaucratic structure that was reproduced on a smaller scale at the provincial courts of its appointed governors. Its religious demography was complex, encompassing Christians of many persuasions, monophysites, Nestorians, Orthodox, and others; pagans; gnostics; Jews; Mazdeans. Minority religious communities were becoming more clearly organized and isolated. The population included priests; traders and merchants; landlords (dihqans), sometimes living not on the land but as absentees in the cities; pastoralists; and large numbers of peasant agriculturalists. In southern Iraq, especially in and around towns like Al-hirah, it included migratory and settled Arabs as well. Both empires relied on standing armies for their defense and on agriculture, taxation, conquest, and trade for their resources. [65]

When the Muslim conquests began, the Byzantines and Sassanians had been in conflict for a century; in the most recent exchanges, the Sassanians had established direct rule in al-hirah, further exposing its many Arabs to their administration. When the Arab conquests began, representatives of Byzantine and Sassanian rule on Arabia's northern borders were not strong enough to resist. [65]

In 622 AD, Mohammed was becoming too powerful in the city of Mecca, and he and 70 of his followers in Mecca were forced to flee to the city of Yathrib, now known as Medina. 622 is the beginning of the Muslim calendar. In 630, Mohammed returned to Mecca with his army and conquered it. Mohammed died in 632, but his successors turned their attention to the Byzantines and the Sassanids.

24.2. The last Sassanian king, Yazdgird III

The last Sassanian king, Yazdgird III, ascended to throne in 632 AD, when he was only eight years old. He ruled during the time of the Muslim invasion of the Sassanian Empire and had to move from province to province in order to gather resources and be able to fight against the invading Arabs. During 629 to 630 AD, the Sassanian Empire had suffered the loss of Yemen, Oman, and Bahrain. [60]

In 633 AD the Sassanian army was defeated by the Muslim army at the battle of D'at al-Salasel. More defeats followed and by 634 AD, Sawad (the name used in early Islamic times for southern Iraq) came under Muslim control. In 636 AD at the battle of Madar, Sassanian forces completely lost southern Mesopotamia to the Arab army. Finally in 637 AD the battle of Qadisiya took place in which the Iranian general Rustam i Farroxzad and most of his army were killed. The king fled the capital, but by 640 AD, the Arabs had taken over the heartland of Iran. After further defeats, Yazdgird III is believed to have been murdered by a local miller near Marw in 651 AD. And that was the official end of the Sassanids, and the last of the ancient Persian empires. [60]

Although all of these details are of interest, there are still many mysteries. After the ultimate defeat of the Sassanians in the last crucial years of the war with the Byzantines (621–628 AD) — itself a tremendously perplexing question — a sociopolitical upheaval unprecedented in the world of late antiquity began: the Arab conquest of the Near East. While the event truncated Byzantium beyond recognition by the 640s, its consequences were even more dire for the Sassanians. For with the death of the last Sassanian king, Yazdgird III (632–651), in the aftermath of the Arab conquest of Iran, came the end of more than a millennium of Iranian rule in substantial sections of the Near East. The Sassanian empire was toppled and swallowed up by the Arab armies. What had happened? Why was an empire that was poised for the dominion of the Near East in 620, when successfully engaging the powerful Byzantines, utterly defeated by 650 by the forces of a people hitherto under its suzerainty, the Arab armies? [61]

Historical research on these questions is ongoing, with no definitive answers.

24.3. The Caliphs versus the Imams

Once Mohammed (570-632) died in 632 AD, there were internecine conflicts among the various Muslim tribes. Mohammed himself had been from the Quraysh tribe, and he apparently made some remarks during his lifetime that his successors should also be from the Quraysh tribe. Needless to say, the other tribes were not willing to accept this. Tribal jealousy is a constant throughout all time and history, usually resulting in slaughter, torture and wars.

What's more interesting is to understand the justifications and excuses that are given for the tribal jealousy and wars. And the succession debates that took place after Mohammed's death are still highly relevant to Iran today.

The debate was over the terms "prophethood" and "caliphate." "Prophethood" referred to the job of carrying on Mohammed's religious ministry, pronouncing judgment what is or is not Allah's will. "Caliphate" refers to politics and government, and the person who will be the political leader. It's the same "separating Church and State" argument that still goes on today. [63]

Mohammed himself had been all-in-one — a religious leader, a military leader, and a political leader. The direct descendants of Mohammed (the future Shias) insisted that Mohammed had already decided that this should continue, and all future Muslim leaders should be direct descendants of Mohammed, and should combine all the functions — religious, military and political — into a single leader. [63]

It took decades and the spilling of much blood to resolve this dispute. In fact, the dispute hasn't been resolved to this day, as we'll see. For now, we'll summarize the situation by saying that the Sunni Muslims had Caliphs but no religious leaders besides individual clerics. The Shias had individual clerics called Imams, but no Caliphs — until Iran's recent Supreme Leaders Khomeini and Khamenei decided to declare that a Supreme Leader was both an Imam and a Caliph. We'll discuss this further in the chapter on Shia theology and "The Guardianship of the Jurist."

By the tenth century, mainstream Shia theology had settled on the belief that there had been 12 infallible Imams, all of them descendants of Mohammed. This theology was the direct result of the disappearance of Imam Muhammad Al-Mahdi in 940 AD. As this was the last direct descendant of Mohammed, there was no 13th Imam to succeed him, and so, according to Shia theology, an "occultation" occurred in 940 — al-Mahdi is still alive, but in hiding. The possible return of al-Mahdi as the messiah to avenge injustices to the Shia is a dominant feature of Iran's politics today.

24.4. The first Shia Imam: Ali Ibn Abi Talib (601-661)

Ali Ibn Abi Talib (601-661), known simply as Ali, was the husband of Mohammed's daughter Fatima az-Zahra (609-632) by his first wife Khadijah (555-619), and was therefore the son-in-law of Mohammed, as well as Mohammed's close companion. Fatima was the second woman in all Arabia to accept Islam, the first being Khadija. They are both considered models for all Muslim women. [64]

Ali's mother was Fatima bint Asad (555-626), who is a different Fatima than his wife. Fatima bint Asad was also the aunt of Mohammed by a different family connection: She married her cousin, Abu Talib ibn Abd al-Muttalib (539-613). The two of them were Ali's parents, but Mohammed himself was Abu Talib's nephew, making Fatima bint Asad and Abu Talib his aunt and uncle. Mohammed himself came to live in their house in 579, after he was orphaned at age eight, so Mohammed and Ali grew up together.

Since Ali and Mohammed grew up in the same household, they were like brothers, and they fought side-by-side in many of the battles in Medina and Mecca. Mohammed had designated Ali as his successor, but vicious tribal politics made that impossible when Mohammed died in 632.

The first compromise Caliph was Abu Bakr (573-634). He was only slightly younger than Mohammed himself, but was the father of Aishah bint Abi Bakr (605-678), one of Mohammed's wives, and was one of Mohammed's closest companions throughout his lifetime. He was the first Caliph (632-634) following Mohammed's death, but died in 634.

Of particular significance during the Abu Bakr's time as Caliph was the Battle of Yamama in December 632. Abu Bakr's army won the battle, but among the dead were 450 "memorizers" (Hafids) of the Koran. Up to this point, there was no official document containing the Koran, and knowledge the various sura and verses was left to the companions of Mohammed who had heard his utterances and memorized them. The loss of such a large number of memorizers motivated Abu Bakr and his successor Umar to appoint a committee to create a written collection suras and verses. We'll return to this subject later when we discuss the disputes over the authenticity of the Koran. [92]

Umar I (584-644) had been designated by Abu Bakr as his successor. Umar had been senior companion to Mohammed and one of hi earliest and staunchest supporters, and, like Ali, was close to Mohammed his whole life. Mohammed married his daughter Hafsa bint Umar (606-665) in 625, and was the second husband to her.

The Battle of Qadisiyya (636) was fought during Umar's caliphate. This was the seminal climax in the conquest of Mohammed's Arab forces over the Sassanid Persian empire.

Uthman ibn Affan (577-656) succeeded Umar as Caliph in 644, and was assassinated in 656, as will be discussed further below. [68] [67]

Within 25 years Muslim Arab forces created the first empire to permanently link western Asia with the Mediterranean. Within another century Muslim conquerors surpassed the achievement of Alexander the Great, not only in the durability of their accomplishment but in its scope as well, reaching from the Iberian Peninsula to Central Asia. Resistance was generally slight and nondestructive, and conquest through capitulation was preferred to conquest by force. After Sassanian Al-hirah fell in 633, a large Byzantine force was defeated in Syria, opening the way to the final conquest of Damascus in 636. The next year further gains were made in Sassanian territory, especially at the Battle of al-Qadisiyyah, and in the next the focus returned to Syria and the taking of Jerusalem. By 640 Roman control in Syria was over, and by 641 the Sassanians had lost all their territory west of the Zagros. During the years 642 to 646 Egypt was taken under the leadership of 'Amr ibn al-'aS, who soon began raids into what the Muslims called the Maghrib, the lands west of Egypt. Shortly thereafter, in the east, Persepolis fell; in 651 the defeat and assassination of the last Sassanian emperor, Yazdegerd III, marked the end of the 400-year-old Sassanian empire. [65]

24.5. The Hashim clan versus the Umayya clan

When Mohammed's army traveled from Medina to complete the conquest of Mecca in 630 AD, it was the climax of a major tribal and clan civil war. From the point of view of generational theory, all civil wars, including this one, follow certain patterns. The main problem is that when the war ends, the two sides still have to live with one another as neighbors in the same communities, and memories of the atrocities committed during the war live on. One side may have reluctantly accepted being subdued by the other side during the war, but when their children grow up, they often don't accept that result. Typically, this results in young people demonstrating, rioting, violence, and acts of terrorism.

There were many tribes and clans involved in the civil war that climaxed in Mecca in 630, but we'll just focus on one tribe and two clans. The tribe is the Quraysh tribe, which is the tribe that controlled Mecca for centuries.

The two clans are from the Quraysh tribe: Banu Hashim (Sons of Hashim) and Banu Umayya (Sons of Umayya).

So to understand the outcome of the assassination of Uthman in 656, we have to understand a little bit of what happened, centuries earlier, when the Hashim and Umayya clans were formed.

The history of these two clans is quite dramatic.

A man named Abd Manaf ibn Qusai (born 430 AD), was the son of Qusay (400-480), the leading member of the Quraysh tribe at the time. Abd Manaf also became a leading member of the Quraysh tribe.

Abd Manaf had two sons, Hashim (464-497) and Abd Shams. According to what may well be a legend, they were conjoined twins (Siamese twins), with Hashim's leg attached to Abd Shams' forehead:

> "Abd Munaf had two sons that were born twins (both of them were born joint together – Siamese twins) and were thus split apart by a sword. One was given the name Haashim, whilst the other was named Umay 'ya [Abd Shams]. Both these families became very well known in Arabia.

There were always feuds that took place between both these families. They always raised their swords against one another and many in each family were killed during these feuds.

After both these twin brothers were separated through the use of a sword, the astrologers of Arabia predicted that Abd Munaf had committed a grave error when he separated both of them by means of a sword. That which he had done was not regarded by them as a good omen.

They said that the descendants of both the Haashim and the Umay'ya families would continue to fight each other in the future.

These predictions did however seem very true, word for word.

If true, the astrologers may have gotten it right. [66]

Hashim (464-497) gave his name to the Banu Hashim clan. This clan gave birth to Mohammed, and the Hashim clan eventually became the Shias.

Abu Shams had a son named Umayya ibn Abd Shams, whose name was given to the Banu Umayya clan. This clan eventually became the Sunnis.

Mohammed's conquest of Mecca in 630 was, at its core, a war between the Hashim and Umayya clans, which later became the Shias and the Sunnis, respectively. Thus, according to one legend, the Shia-Sunni split in the 600's was caused in the 400s, when a man committed a grave error, separating his two conjoined twins sons with a sword, which was a bad omen.

24.6. Ali becomes Caliph (656): Partisans of Ali = Shiat Ali = Shia

The next five years following the assassination of Uthman were highly significant, because they established the Sunni-Shia split, and also established power centers in Damascus Syria for the Arabs, and Kufa Iraq (near the border of today's Iran) for the Persians. It was this five years that laid the groundwork for Islam for centuries to come.

Following the death of Mohammed in 632, there was a scramble to decide on a successor Caliph. As previously described, Abu Bakr and Umar I were compromise choices designed to preserve unity. They were not Mohammed's first choice for successor, Ali (Ibn Abi Talib), but they were both close companions of Mohammed and had fought with Mohammed, and they were both from the Hashim clan.

When Umar I died in 644, two Hashimites had been chosen as Caliph. It's therefore not surprising that the next caliph was an Umayyad. Uthman ibn Affan (577-656), an Umayyad, was chosen by a small committee to be the new Caliph.

By this time, the first generation of young people growing up after Mohammed's victory were beginning to make their voices heard, and the old Hashim-Umayya rivalries flared in the form of anti-Uthman protests. There was discontent over how he was chosen. Once in office, he was accused of nepotism — favoring his own family and the Umayyad clan. When conquests occurred, he favored a system where only people in Medina could distribute the wealth from the conquests, even if they occurred elsewhere. [65] [63]

Possibly the most "objectionable" of Uthman's actions is his control over the creation of the Koran as a written collection of "Recitations of Mohammed." He ordered that all other collections be destroyed, infuriating the communities where those collections had been made. We'll be discussing issues surrounding the written Koran in a later chapter. [65]

It's not known who Uthman's assassin was, but it's clear that Uthman had a lot of enemies, and a young person from any of those other clans and communities could have been motivated to do it.

The assassination of Uthman in 656 was a tremendous shock to the entire Muslim community, as any horrible event always is, the first time that it happens.

Finally, Ali was selected as the new Caliph. He was the winner of a three-way contest:

- Ali was supported by Ali's party in Iraq. These were the "Partisans of Ali" or "Shiat Ali" or "Shia." This became the Shia branch of Islam.
- Muawiya (602-680), the governor of Syria in Damascus, was supported by Uthman's clan, the Umayyas. This became the Sunni branch of Islam.
- Aishah bint Abi Bakr (605-678), Mohammed's second and youngest wife, led a coalition of other clans from the Quraysh tribe, supported by other powerful families in Mecca.

Ali was chosen as Caliph, but this only triggered more factional warfare among the Muslim community.

24.7. The Battle of Siffin (657) and the Kharijites and 'infidel' concept

Ali was Caliph, but there was still bitter hostility between Ali's Hashim clan and Muawiya's Umayya clan. Ali, the Shia leader, was in Kufa, while Muawiya, the Sunni leader, was in Damascus. They prepared their respective armies for battle, and the armies met at the village of Siffin, near today's Raqqa in Syria.

Ali's army was winning, but Muawiya's army pulled an incredible stunt. 500 of Muawiya's fighters put copies of the Koran on the tips of their spears. Ali's fighters were in shock when they saw this, and they halted the fighting, allowing Muawiya's forces to escape. This outcome was considered to have been a disaster for all of Shia Islam [74]

Ali's shocked generals wanted to agree to a demand by Muawiya to submit their disagreements to "Arbitration." Many of Ali's partisans in Kufa were opposed to this, instead favoring continuing the war to victory. But Ali, who was in a generation that has seen repeated crisis wars, was a compromiser, and he agreed to the Arbitration. As a result, Muawiya escaped defeat and also emboldened Muawiya. [63]

To walk away from a fight like this is a very serious matter at any place and time, and in this case it split Ali's partisans. We talk about two major Muslim sects at this time — the Sunnis and the Shias — but there was also a third one, the Kharijites (the "seceders").

The Kharijites sect were only in existence for about five centuries, but their ideas have tremendous impact today because they serve as a model for today's most extreme and violent jihadis. The Kharijites justified their extremism by a religious argument that is heard today from extreme jihadists: According to the Kharijites, judgments can only be made by Allah by winning a battle, so that Allah can make the decision by bringing about a victory in battle by one side or the other. Any men who use "Arbitration" are infidels, because they're making a decision that only Allah should make, and then only in battle. [63]

24.8. Abdullah ibn Saba and the alleged Jewish origins of Shia Islam

One of the controversies within Islam is the claim that the Shia sect was started by Abdullah ibn Saba, a Jew who pretended to convert to Islam and who then provoked hostilities that led to the Sunni-Shia split. [69]

Let's start by saying that there is no chance whatsoever that this conclusion is true. The Sunni-Shia split was based on centuries of ethnic war between two tribes, the Umayyads and the Hashimites, and the split would have occurred with 100% certainty, whether Abdullah ibn Saba had ever existed or not — and there are many historians who believe that he did not exist.

According to this story, the Jews of Yathrib (Medina) did not want to see the Arab tribes unified, so they made various attempts to subvert Islam from the inside to create schisms. A group of Jewish conspirators, it is said, responsible for the assassination of Umar, the second Caliph. Next, Umar's son Ubaidallah got revenge by killing some of the Jews.

Uthman then became Caliph, and put Ubaidallah on trial. Ali Ibn Abi Talib, who years later would become the first Shia Imam, advised Uthman to charge Ubaidallah with murder, and have him executed. However, sympathizers of Ubaidallah convinced Uthman to show mercy, because he had acted out of distress when his father died.

This infuriated the Jewish conspirators, especially Abdullah ibn Saba, who pretended to convert to Islam, and planned to destroy Islam from within.

The story continues that the Zoroastrians (of the defeated Persian Empire), the Christians (of the defeated Eastern Roman Empire), and the Jews (who had been expelled by the Muslims) grieved for the old days. The Jewish Abdullah ibn Saba used these grievances to sow discontent against Uthman. He started by claiming that Ali should have become Caliph, but that the three Caliphs had usurped this right. [69]

Ibn Saba created a secret Saba'ite cult, and captivated followers, who were mostly pagans, by glorifying Ali, saying that he had powers above those of a human being, and by infusing Zoroastrian beliefs into Islam. One belief in particular was that God's spirit moves from one leader to the next, through his descendants, which became a core belief of Shia Islam in the form of the 12 infallible Imams, which we will discuss in later chapters on Shia Islam theology. This cult filled the ranks of the Shiat Ali (partisans of Ali).

Ali himself didn't realize what was happening until it was too late. The Saba'ite cult assassinated Uthman. Ali did not take part in this, nor did he approve of it, but it resulted in the creation of the Shia sect, according to the story. [69]

This story might have been forgotten today, but it has been adopted by the jihadist group, the so-called Islamic State (IS or ISIS or ISIL or Daesh). A statement issued by ISIS in January 2016 says the following:

> "Initiated by a sly Jew [Abdullah ibn Saba], [the Shia] are an apostate sect drowning in worship of the dead, cursing the best companions and wives of the Prophet, spreading doubt on the very basis of the religion (the Koran and the Sunnah), defaming the very honor of the Prophet, and preferring their "twelve" imams to the prophets and even to Allah! ... Thus, the Rafidah [another word for Shias] are mushrik [polytheist] apostates who must be killed wherever they are to be found, until no Rafidi walks on the face of earth, even if the jihad claimants despise such."

Thus, the story (or legend) of the sly Jew, Abdullah ibn Saba, lives on even today, as an ISIS tool to justify killing women and children in the name of their perverted beliefs.

24.9. Shia-Sunni clashes become vicious after Ali is assasinated (661)

The Kharijites became as fanatical as today's jihadist extremists. They plotted a terrorist attack in 661 to simultaneously assassinate both Ali in Kufa and Muawiya in Damasacus. Muawiya was only slightly wounded, but Ali was fatally wounded. Before he died, he designated his 37-year-old son al-Hasan (Al-Hasan ibn Ali ibn Abi Talib, 624-670) as his successor.

Ali's partisans (the Shias) were devastated by the war with Muawiya (the Sunnis) and by the secession of the Kharijites. To avoid further bloodshed, Al-Hasan signed a peace agreement with Muawiya, passing the role of Caliph to Muawiya, in return for guarantees that there would be no discrimination against Shias. The agreement also specified that on the death of Muawiya, al-Hasan would become Caliph again if he were still alive. [74]

Sunni and Shia histories seem to agree that Muawiya ignored his commitments, even terrorizing or killing innocent Shias. Muawiya wanted his own son Yazid (Yazid ibn Muawiya ibn Abi Sufyan, 647-683) to become Caliph to succeed himself, and arranged for al-Hasan to be poisoned and killed in 670, so that he would not outlive Muawiya.

Muawiya lived until early 680, at which time his son Yazid became the new Caliph.

Ali's brother al-Husayn (Al-Husayn ibn Ali ibn Abi Talib, 626-680) became the new leader of the Shias, and remained so until he was killed at the Battle of Karbala in 680.

Chapter 25. Battle of Karbala (October 10, 680) and beheading of al-Husayn

The Battle of Karbala was a small, one-day battle between the Shias and the Sunnis, but it resulted in the massacre of an entire family of the grandson of Mohammed, including the beheading of Mohammed's grandson al-Husayn, and so today it is considered the seminal battle that defined the Shia-Sunni split for millennia to come.

25.1. Prelude to the Battle of Karbala

After al-Hasan was poisoned and killed in 670, the leadership of the Shias was taken over by Ali's brother al-Husayn (Al-Husayn ibn Ali ibn Abi Talib, 626-680). Sunni leader Muawiya was still recognized by both Sunnis and Shias as the Caliph of all Muslims, but relations between the Sunnis and the Shias remained bitter and violent.

25.2. The Battle of Karbala

Muawiya died early in 680, and his son Yazid became Caliph. The Shia community, centered in the city of Kufa, Iraq, felt that al-Husayn should be Caliph, and the leaders in Kufa agreed and invited al-Husayn to take refuge with them, promising to have him proclaimed caliph there. Al-Husayn set out from Mecca with all his family and retainers, expecting to be received with enthusiasm by the citizens of Kufa. However, Muawiya had become aware of the invitation, and sent word to the chiefs of Kufa that there would be reprisal if they supported al-Husayn. When al-Husayn arrived in Karbala, about 100 miles from Kufa, he was met by a large army of perhaps 4,000 men under the command of the son of the founder of Kufa. Al-Husayn had only 72 fighting men, and received none of the promised aid from Kufa. His family and followers were almost all killed, and their bodies mutilated. [75]

25.3. Aftermath and the commemoration of Ashura

This event had an explosive emotional impact on the Shia community. The perception was that Al-Husayn ibn Ali ibn Abi Talib, the grandson of Mohammed and perhaps the holiest man alive at that time, had been killed, beheaded and mutilated, along with his family, because his supposedly devout partisans in Kufa had betrayed him by promising to provide aid, and then abandoning him when he most needed that aid. [75]

Although the Shia-Sunni split had begun in 656, there had been at least a pretense of unity since then. But with the Battle of Karbala, all pretense was gone. Yazid and many Sunni leaders were regarded as murderers, and their names have ever since been held as accursed by Shia Muslims. The tomb in Karbala of the decapitated martyr al-Husayn is Shia Islam's most holy place. [75]

Ashura is the holiest day of the year in the Shia calendar, commemorating the death of al-Husayn. It is roughly equivalent in importance to the Easter holiday and 40 days of penance in Lent in Christianity, commemorating the death and resurrection of Christ.

Ashura is not a day of celebration, but a day of atonement for Shia Muslims in Iran and around the world. It's a religious festival marked by 10 days of mourning, in which many devotees whip and cut themselves with chains and knives and some drive knives into their scalps and is seen as a way of washing away their sins. The symbolic use of blood appears to be gory to outsiders, but to the Shia Muslims in countries around the world, it's a way of atoning for allowing the death of al-Husayn. [76]

On the other side, Yazid in Damascus was an Umayyad Caliph whose army had defeated the army of the insurgent Shias, and this secured the position of the Umayyad dynasty until it was defeated by the Iranian Abbasids in 750.

25.4. Hussaini Brahmans - the link between Shia Muslims and Hindus

There is a community of Hindus in India today that claim a link to Shia Muslims through the Battle of Karbala. Historical accounts say that Rahab Dutt (Rahib Datt), an old man from Lahore who traded with Arabia in those days, had promised Mohammed to stand by his grandson in his fight to uphold the truth. The result was that Dutt and his seven sons fought on the side of al-Husayn at the Battle of Karbala. According to the story, the swordsmen stood their ground till they were felled by hundreds of horsemen. [78]

Today, Dutt's community are known as Hussaini Brahmans. The community lived in Lahore until the Partition war in 1947, and currently live in east Delhi. [79]

The Hussaini Brahmans are one part of a large and close historical relationship between Hindus of India and Shia Muslims of Iran. This close relationship was emphasized in 2016 when India and Iran signed a deal to develop the Port of Chabahar in Iran, to be used for commercial shipping between India and Central Asia, without having to travel through Pakistan. [104]

During the visit by India's prime minister Narendra Modi to Tehran, Modi gave a speech that emphasized the long relationship between the two cultures:

> "Centuries of free exchange of ideas and traditions, poets and craftsmen, art and architecture, culture and commerce have enriched both our civilizations. Our heritage has also been a source of strength and economic growth for our nations. The richness of Persian heritage is an integral part of the fabric of the Indian society. A part of Iranian culture lives in Indian hearts. And, a slice of Indian heritage is woven into the Iranian society. Our ancient heroes and epics bear striking parallels. The dargahs of Azmer Sharif and Hazrat Nizamuddin in India are equally revered in Iran. Mahabharata and Shahnama, Bhima and Rustam, Arjuna and Arsh exhibit similarity in our world views and values. ...
>
> India and Iran have always been partners and friends. Our historical ties may have seen their share of ups and downs. But, throughout our partnership has remained a source of boundless strength for both of us. Time has come for us to regain the past glory of traditional ties and links. Time has come for us to march together. [104] "

Chapter 26. Expansion of the Islamic empire

26.1. Birth and death of empires — the cycles of history

By the mid-600s, the Mideast and surrounding regions had seen several huge empires, each one being conquered by the next one, in the unending cycles of history.

With the Arab conquest of the Sassanid empire in the mid 600s, there began the expansion of the Islamic empire, through a series of military conquests.

By 750, the Umayyad dynasty had already conquered an enormous region stretching from Spain to North Africa to Arabia and Iran. There were Islamic administrative centers in Cordoba in Spain, Kairouan in Tunisia (northern Africa - Maghreb), al-Fustat in Egypt, Damascus in Syria, Kufa in Iraq, Medina and Mecca in Arabia, and Isfahan in Iran.

When the Abbasids conquered the Umayyads in 750, it was not the end of the Islamic empire. To the contrary, it was just a change in political leadership in an empire that continued to grow.

The military conquests continued rapidly in a long period during which the conquest of the hearts and minds of the majority of the subject population also occurred. Between 634 and 870 Islam was transformed from the badge of a small Arab ruling class to the dominant faith of a vast empire that stretched from the western Mediterranean into Central Asia. As a result of this long and gradual period of conversion, Arab cultures intermingled with the indigenous cultures of the conquered peoples to produce Islam's fundamental orientations and identities. The Arabic language became a vehicle for the transmission of high culture, even though the Arabs remained a minority; for the first time in the history of the region around the Middle East, a new language of high culture, carrying a great cultural florescence, replaced all previous languages of high culture. Trade and taxation replaced booty as the fiscal basis of the Muslim state; a nontribal army replaced a tribal one; and a centralized empire became a nominal confederation, with all of the social dislocation and rivalries those changes imply. [65]

26.2. Zaydi Shia Muslims

After the Umayyads won at the Battle of Karbala, there were a series of Umayyad Caliphs. At the same time, there was a great deal of unrest throughout the empire controlled by the Umayyads, including a number of minor rebellions that were suppressed.

One special rebellion must be mentioned because it's highly relevant to today's news.

In 740, Zayd Ibn Ali led an rebellion against the Umayyad caliph. The rebellion was put down, but Zayd's followers remained as a community, and in 893 established a Zaydi state in today's Yemen. The Zaydis ruled in northern Yemen for over a millennium, until 1962. Some 400 Zaydi tribes live in the rugged mountains of northern Yemen, with a total of some five million members. For over one thousand years they have been the dominant community in the Yemen, fighting against Sunnis and Shias alike. [77]

The Zaydis are today's Houthis, an Iran-backed group fighting against the internationally recognized government backed by Saudi Arabia and United Arab Emirates (UAE). They're considered to be Shias, even though theologically they're considered halfway between Sunnis and Shias, leaning a bit in the direction of the Sunnis. They're called "Fivers" because of their allegiance to the fifth Shia Imam (as opposed to the Iranians, who are "Twelvers"). See the discussion of Imams in a later chapter. [65]

26.3. The Battle of Zab (750) and the Abbasids

One rebellion in particular was successful. The Abbasids were a tribe in Khorasan in northwestern Iran and today's Turkmenistan, with a name derived from that of Abbas ibn Abd al-Muttalib, the uncle of the prophet Mohammed.

Starting from about 718, during the generational awakening era, the Abbasids, with the support of Shia Arabs and Persians in Khorasan, used propaganda and political means to attack the Umayyads. Open revolt began in 747, under the leadership of Abu Muslim of the Abu Hashim clan. The Abbasids took Kufa in 749, and defeated the Umayyad forces in January 750 in the climactic Battle of the Great Zab River in Mesopotamia. [81]

26.4. The Banquet of Blood (750)

There is one story called "The Banquet of Blood," almost certainly apocryphal, which may have been the inspiration for a Game of Thrones television episode. The details are vague. Later in the year 750, the Abbasids wanted to finish off the remaining members of the Umayyad family once and for all. The Abbasids invited 80 Umayyad family members to a grand feast in the Palestinian town of abu-Futrus, on the pretext of a reconciliation between the two families. According to the story, once the feasting and festivities were done, almost all of the princes were remorselessly clubbed to death by the Abbasid followers, and then the feasting continued over their dead bodies – thus eliminating the possibility of Umayyad return to caliphate power. [80]

26.5. The Abbasid Dynasty (750-1258)

There were two great dynasties of caliphs and caliphates in the history of Islam — the Umayyad Dynasty and the Abbasid Dynasty. [81]

By 750, the Umayyad dynasty had already conquered an enormous region stretching from Spain to North Africa to Arabia and Iran. After 750, the Islamic world was no longer unified in a single caliphate. Instead, local dynasties in Egypt, North Africa, Spain and elsewhere claimed status as a caliphate. [81]

After the Abbasids took power following the Battle of Zab, they moved the capital to the new city of Baghdad. The primary focus of the Umayyads had been westward, but the Abbasids' focus was eastward — to Persia and Central Asia (Transoxania). The Abbasid dynasty finally fell in 1258 during a Mongol siege of Baghdad. [81]

Part VII. The Koran and Sharia (Islamic) law

Chapter 27. Development of Sharia law following Mohammed's death

When Mohammed died in 632, Islam consisted of a small group of Arabs in Medina and Mecca. From 634 to 870, conquests first by the armies of Mecca, then by the armies of the Umayyad dynasty, and then by the armies of the Abbasid dynasty, transformed Islam from this small Arab ruling class into the dominant faith of a vast empire that stretched from Spain and the western Mediterranean into Central Asia. [65]

Ruling a growing empire is not an easy task. It requires setting up administrative procedures for collecting taxes, rules for marriage and children, resolution of contract disputes, punishments for crimes, boundaries for internal groups, rules for trade and tariffs between internal groups, and so forth. Ideally, this would be accomplished by a comprehensive written system of laws that could be referenced by any local or regional leader in the empire.

Unfortunately the Koran provided little help. Once Mohammed's followers had fled in 622 from Mecca to Medina (the Hijra), he became the head of a state, and his utterances as recorded in the Koran were mainly concerned with public business. However, this was no comprehensive system of law, but rather was series of provisional solutions to a ceaseless succession of emergencies. These utterances could have been used by subsequent leaders to resolve similar local issues, but would not be of much help in governing an empire. [82]

The Roman Empire and the Byzantine Empire had already been dealing for centuries with the problems of governing a huge empire, and so it's natural that Muslims would have adopted much of Roman Law, rather than figure things out from a blank slate. It's reasonable to assume that Sharia (Islamic) law is a merger of Roman Law, Mohammed's utterances, and *ad hoc* solutions to local problems devised by local leaders. We must also include Jewish law in this list of sources. We'll make the assumption in this text that Sharia law is a merger of all of these sources, and leave it to the scholars to decide what percentage of Sharia law can be assigned to each of these four categories of sources. [82]

Chapter 28. Roman Law versus Sharia (Islamic) law: The role of the Jurist

Western countries in general have adopted some derivative of Roman law. We intend to focus on one aspect of Roman law as implemented in the west — separation of Church and State — and contrast this aspect with Sharia law.

In their daily lives, Westerners have two sets of laws to deal with, and either one may apply to any situation. For example, eating a meal in a restaurant is regulated by civil laws having to do with rules for purchase and tax collection, rules for how food is prepared, and whether the food is safe. But there's a whole separate set of regulations that can vary from person to person depending on his religion. For example, Hindus may not eat beef, while Muslims and Jews may not eat pork. So there are two sets of laws, civil and religious laws, and they're kept separate to the greatest extent possible.

There are some crossovers between religious and secular side, even in Western Roman law. Just looking at the Biblical Ten Commandments reveals some confusion. The commandment "You shall have no other gods before me" is clearly a religious command. But "You shall not murder" and "You shall not steal" are clearly on the civic side. The commandments "Honor your father and your mother" and "You shall not commit adultery" are neither religious nor civic or, arguably, they are on the boundary between the religious and the civic.

But Sharia law is a complete legal system, not limited to just civil or religious aspects of life. Under Islam, all human behavior is in some manner religious. Therefore, there is always a moral and immoral way of acting. There are five classifications of behavior:

- Wajib, actions obligatory on Believers
- Matlub, desirable or recommended (but not obligatory) actions
- Mubah, indifferent actions
- Makruh, actions objectionable but not forbidden
- Haram, prohibited actions

These five categories apply to all human actions — contractual obligations, property, family law, criminal law, administrative law, etc. The religion of Islam and the government form one body. [83]

Both Roman and Sharia law share the concept of a "jurist" or "judge." This is someone who has received proper training and recognition, and is empowered to resolve disputes, and even to make new law, when no existing law applies to a situation.

A jurist in Roman law reaches decisions by referring to legislated law, political regulations, and precedents reached by other judges. A jurist in Sharia law refers to these same sources, but these sources are subordinate to the highest authority, the Koran, and to Mohammed's utterances as passed down through sunnah and hadith narratives.

It's worth pointing out that legislated law can be changed at any time by the legislature, regulations can be changed at any time by the politicians, and laws defined by precedent can be changed at any time by an equal or higher court (jurist) setting a different precedent.

But in Sharia law, the recorded utterances of Mohammed are fixed.

Chapter 29. There's no such thing as Sharia law

When I say that there's no such thing as Sharia law, I mean that it's the same as Roman law — there's no fixed body of Sharia law, and it can be changed almost at will by politicians in different countries.

29.1. Misunderstandings about Sharia law

Today, there's a great deal of hysteria and ignorance in the West related to Sharia law. Statements like "Sharia law oppresses women because it requires them to wear headscarves" or "Sharia law says that infidels have to be killed" are deeply ignorant, and yet are widely believed in the West.

Let's take the headscarf example. Is a headscarf required by Sharia law or not? In Turkey under Ataturk, a headscarf was illegal. In Turkey under Recep Tayyip Erdogan, a headscarf is sometimes allowed and sometimes required. In Iran under the Shah, a headscarf was not required. After the 1979 civil war and the rise to power of Supreme Leaders Khomeini and Khamenei, a headscarf is required. In Egypt, a headscarf is optional. All of these countries are governed by Sharia or Islamic law. So which is it? Does Sharia law require a headscarf, allow a headscarf, or forbid a headscarf? Which of those is Sharia law? The answer is that all of them are Sharia law, because Sharia law can be anything that any politician wants it to be.

The second example is claims, usually by extremist Sunni jihadists, that Sharia law requires that all "infidels" be killed. That this is false is proven by the fact that there are many Muslim-majority countries today, governed by Sharia law, where people of other religions are not killed and, in fact, where killing someone of another religion is treated as murder. Is killing Christians and Jews part of Sharia law? If so, then why aren't Muslim governments around the world killing Christians and Jews? The only ones killing Christians and Jews are extremist jihadists who are purposely defiling and blackening Sharia law for their own purposes.

The ironic thing about this whole issue is that even extremist jihadists are killing few Christians and Jews. The number of Christians and Jews they kill is minuscule compared to the number of Muslims they kill. If you look at the figures, the number of Christians killed by jihadists is minuscule — less than 2% --- compared to the total number of people killed by jihadists. Overwhelmingly, the people being killed by jihadists are other Muslims. [105]

In fact, many things in the Koran contradict the claims made by extremist jihadists. It's well-known that Mohammed himself held Jews and Christians in very high regard as "people of the Book," and through history Muslim governments have taxed them, not killed them. Finally, it's worth noting that the Koran (sura 4:29) says, "And do not kill yourselves," which would suggest that suicide bombers are an extreme violation of Sharia law.

What about prayers? You'd think that something so fundamental to Islam would be unambiguously specified by Sharia law.

Well, it is true that all Muslims are required to pray five times per day. But Sunnis are required to have no less than one hour between prayers, while Shias are allowed to consolidate their prayers into three groups. Some Muslims are required to fold their hands over their chests while praying, while others hold their hands at their sides. Sunnis consider self-flagellation to be a very major sin, while Shias use self-flagellation on the Ashura commemoration of the Battle of Karbala. [84]

So whether the issue is headscarves, killing infidels, or prayer styles, the popular Western view that Sharia law is a fixed body of law that all Muslims follow is no more valid than to say that Roman law is a fixed body of law that all Westerners follow.

29.2. Mohammed's wives, and accusations of polygamy and pedophilia

Jesus Christ had no descendants, with the result that there are no controversies in Christianity related to his descendants.

But for Islam, the descendants of Mohammed play an overwhelmingly important role. And since anything having to do with women, sex and marriage is always controversial in any culture, it's not surprising that there are cultural issues surrounding Mohammed's wives and children.

The most obvious example is niqabs or burkas that cover a woman's entire body, hiding her figure and her hair, sometimes exposing nothing but her eyes. Many Westerners say that the use of niqabs and burkas proves that Islam suppresses women. And yet, many Muslim women voluntarily wear these garments, and like them because they can go out shopping or in public without being stared at, "objectified," or subjected to unwanted male approaches. Furthermore, these garments are not required by Islam, just as Sharia law doesn't require a woman to wear a headscarf.

I recall visiting Germany in the 1970s and being quite shocked to see advertising pictures of bare-breasted models in the shop windows of women's clothing stores. This is something that would never have been permitted in America at that time, or today. It's purely a cultural issue.

And I'm also reminded of the song "At the Big Check Apron Ball" from the 1950s Broadway musical comedy "New Girl In Town." The song contains this verse: "Oh, in these modern days / When ladies show their ankles, / What's there to keep a poor lad, poor lad, / From going simply mad?"

So the point is that women's clothing is a purely cultural issue, and Westerners really have no business criticizing the clothing that Muslim women wear.

So now let's turn to another cultural issue, polygamy.

Mohammed was monogamously married to his first wife Khadijah (555-619) for 25 years, but when she died in 619, Mohammed took on many more wives. Many Westerners criticize Mohammed and Islam itself for polygamy, a criticism that's particularly ironic these days when Western nations seem to permit anyone to marry pretty much anyone else.

In fact, any Western criticism of marriage practices in any other country is pretty laughable, given the high rates of divorce, abuse and prostitution in Western countries. Westerners may criticize marriage practices in Muslim countries, but many Muslims in other countries view marital relations in the West to be a complete mess.

In today's politically correct society, it's easy to forget that polygamy serves a valuable social purpose at times in history when war has killed off many men, leaving many women without partners. In those situations, the only way for most women to receive protection is through polygamous marriages. Furthermore, having a number of unattached women walking around in this kind of society would be very destabilizing, and could get women raped and men killed. So in a society with fewer men than women, polygamy protects women and stabilizes the society as a whole.

This is exactly the situation that obtained in the Arabian peninsula for centuries, where war was a way of life. Many of Mohammed's wives were widows, and there is evidence that many of his marriages were specifically for the protection of the women. At any rate, polygamy is a purely cultural thing, and it's really not for Westerners to criticize in other cultures.

Not all Muslim majority countries permit polygamy, but those that do regulate it. For example, in Malaysia in 1984, Islamic Family Law listed five conditions to be followed by a Muslim wanting more than one wife. The conditions, some of which were subsequently modified, are: [106]

- He must have an appropriate financial situation;
- he must ensure that all wives are kept under the same conditions;
- existing wife or wives shall not be harmed,
- a new marriage shall be "just and necessary",
- a new marriage shall not, either directly or indirectly, lower the standard of living of the existing wife and other dependents.

So polygamy in other cultures can be perfectly reasonable in the right circumstances.

Now let's turn to another issue, that many people consider even more contentious. Apparently, after the death of Mohammed's first wife Khadijah, Mohammed married Aisha bint Abi Bakr (605-678 or 614-678) when she was six years old, but they did not consummate the marriage ("have sex") until she was nine years old, at which time she was considered to be old enough. Mohammed is accused of being a pedophile because of this. [71]

Aisha was the daughter of Abu Bakr (573-634), one of Mohammed's closest companions during his lifetime, and selected as the first Caliph following Mohammed's death. According to contemporary narratives, Mohammed married Aisha at the request of her father.

Today, marriage for a girl under age 15 is illegal in most countries, including Muslim countries, and having sex with a 9 year old girl is shocking to almost everyone. On the other hand, there are often news stories about very young girls being forced into marriage with an older man by their parents, especially if the parents do not have the money or means to provide for their daughters, and want protection for their daughters.

But is it just a cultural issue? Defenders of Mohammed claim that it clearly is. There were no restrictions on marriage by young girls at Mohammed's time, and there weren't until recent times. There were probably many such marriages at the time, and they may well have been justified in the same way that polygamy is justified — the best protection for a girl is to be married, and the best way to keep a society stable is to make sure that there are not many unattached girls and women walking around. Defenders of Mohammed say that today's cultural standards should not be applied to marriages that were common practice at the time of Mohammed. [70]

The government web site girlshealth.gov says that puberty in girls can begin as early as age 8. (It's usually two or three years later for boys.) That indicates that a girl at age 9 is biologically able to have sex, and even get pregnant. [72]

Let me try to explain this another way. As I'm writing this chapter, there are news stories of a BBC investigation in the town of Diepsloot, near Johannesburg, South Africa. According to the report, "This is one of the most dangerous places in Johannesburg. If you are found to be walking at night, you risk your life 100%. Rape is something that is very common, and it can often end in murder too." The 43 minute BBC documentary interviewed not only victims of rape, but also self-confessed rapists who were willing to admit their activities, including rape with total impunity.

There's little doubt that such cultures exist in many places in the world today. Rape with impunity of girls and women is commonplace today wherever there is war or any kind of breakdown in civil control. It's very likely that such a culture also existed at Mohammed's time, in the chaos of war.

So you can ask yourself whether it's plausible that a father like Abu Bakr would ask his close companion Mohammed, whose wife Khadijah had recently died, to marry his very young daughter Aisha, and the answer is that from the father's point of view, there are likely only two choices: let her walk around unattached and risk the almost certain probability of being raped, or marry a man who will love her and take care of her. And it's worth pointing out that a man who rapes a single young girl is committing a crime against someone with little standing, while a man raping a married young girl is committing a crime against the husband, a man who may very well murder the rapist.

The question that is raised is whether a girl at that age is emotionally able to marry and have sex. That judgment is way beyond my skill set, but I take note of the fact that Mohammed always referred to Aisha as his favorite wife and, after he died in 632, Aisha had a long life where she was extremely powerful and respected, dying in 678. As far as I can tell, for Aisha at least, marriage at age 9 resulted in a good life for her. [71]

I've included this discussion of polygamy and pedophilia in this book because I've promised to deal with controversies within Islam in a respectful, balanced and non-ideological way. I hope readers will find this information useful.

Chapter 30. Disputes over the authenticity of the Bible

Many people see both the Bible and the Koran as authentic texts that were written millennia ago and are preserved in their original forms today. Not surprisingly, these views are not correct, and it's interesting to compare a little bit of the histories of the Bible and the Koran.

The earliest copies of the Bible's Old Testament were written on scrolls without vowels or accents. It wasn't until the 5th century AD that Jewish scholars produced an official transcription of the Old Testament, with vowels and accents. In the meantime, the Old Testament was translated into ancient Greek in the 3rd and 2nd centuries BC. These versions contained significant differences from the versions produced by Jewish scholars. Other versions were in the Aramaic and Syriac languages. However, all existing versions were thrown into question and dispute in just the last 50 years, with the discovery of the Dead Sea Scrolls, which are versions of the old Testament books that were written prior to any of those just described. On top of that, the Catholic and Protestant versions of the Old Testament are different, so there is no agreement today on a single version of the Old Testament. [85]

With regard to the New Testament, different versions of the Gospels and other books were used by various Christian communities for the first four centuries AD. During the fourth century there were extremely vitriolic political battles over which books would be in the New Testament. Finally, in 367, a Bishop named Athanasius declared: "In these [27 writings] alone the teaching of godliness is proclaimed. No one may add to them, and nothing may be taken away from them." His recommendations were adopted, and those 27 books were adopted as the official New Testament. [86]

Chapter 31. Brief summary of the Koran

We've briefly described the history of the development of the Bible mainly to compare it to the development of the Koran, and to illustrate where they are similar and different.

No summary of the Koran, particularly a brief summary, could ever convey more than a taste of what the Koran is about. Still, most Westerners are completely unfamiliar with the Koran, so we want to begin by sampling some of the issues that the Koran deals with.

Note that we postpone to a later chapter the issue of violence in the Koran, especially the so-called sword-verses.

A study of the Koran will reveal that just as Islam takes care of such issues like individual devotion and morals, it also deals with the affairs of family, living and family relationship, marriage, divorce, trading and transactions, rearing of children, obedience to "those who are vested with authority," debt, mortgage, war and peace, civil law, penal and criminal laws, international law, and the like. [11]

31.1. Money lending

The longest verse of the Koran is related to money lending and asserts that if you want to lend money to somebody, you have to get written receipt from him in the presence of two witnesses before handing him the money. "If no pen and a sheet of paper are available, take something valuable from him as a mortgage which is to be given back to the borrower when he gives back the money he borrowed." (Koran 2:282-283) [11]

31.2. Verses about marriage, divorce, dower, conjugal life, family disputes

Marriage and divorce also are examples of social issues. There are numerous verses in the Koran about marriage rites and etiquette (Koran 2:240), divorce rites and etiquette (Koran 2:230, 33:49), the rules of payment and acceptance of dower(Koran 4:20), the person whom one is allowed or not allowed to marry (Koran 4:23), conjugal life (Koran 2:222-223), settling family disputes, and others. For example, it states about settling family disputes:

> "And if you fear a split between the two of them, then appoint an arbiter from his relatives and an arbiter from her relatives. If they desire reconcilement, Allah shall reconcile them. Indeed Allah is all-knowing, all-aware." (Koran 4:35) [11]

31.3. Koran verses about inheritance

There are many verses in the Koran devoted to inheritance. For example:

> "Allah enjoins you concerning your children: for the male shall be the like of the share of two females, and if there be [two or] more than two females, then for them shall be two-thirds of what he leaves; but if she be alone, then for her shall be a half. (Koran 4:65) [11]

31.4. The Koran on civil war among the faithful

Civil war may take place at any time. The Koran states:

> "If two groups of the faithful fight one another, make peace between them. But if one party of them aggresses against the other, fight the one which aggresses until it returns to Allah's ordinance. Then, if it returns, make peace between them fairly, and do justice. Indeed Allah loves the just." (Koran 49:9) [11]

31.5. Koran on business dealings and transactions

The Koran specifies the rules and regulations of trading. Here are three examples:

> "Allah has allowed trade and forbidden usury." (Koran 2:275)

> "O you who have faith! When the call is made for prayer on Friday, hurry up toward the remembrance of Allah, and leave all business." (Koran 62:9)

"O you who have faith! Keep your agreements." (Koran 62:9)
[11]

31.6. Koran on theft: cut off their hands

There are numerous laws in the Koran concerning social crimes.
Theft is considered one of the gravest crimes in society:

> "As for the thief, man and woman, cut off their hands as a re-
> quital for what they have earned. [That is] an exemplary pun-
> ishment from Allah and Allah is all-mighty, all-wise."(Koran
> 5:38) [11]

31.7. The Koran on fornication or obscene acts

With regard to committing fornication or obscene acts, when a
Muslim authority or judge discovers that such an act had been committed, it is considered a crime in Islam and a severe penalty is assigned for it even if there is no complainant. The aim is to ensure social immunity from it and foster security against violations.

> "As for the fornicatress and the fornicator, strike each of them
> a hundred lashes, and let not pity for them overcome you in
> Allah's law, if you believe in Allah and the Last Day, and let
> their punishment be witnessed by a group of the faithful."
> (Koran 24:2) [11]

Chapter 32. Disputes over the authenticity of the Koran

We've briefly described the history of the development of the Bible to show how chaotic the development of the Bible was, and how there are still disagreements today about exactly what the Bible is, so the reader should not be surprised to learn that there are similar chaos and disagreements about the development of the Koran, and the subsequent texts in the Sunnah and Hadith.

Jewish and Christian scholars studying the history of Judaism and Christianity have for centuries performed Bible criticism using a variety of analytical methods including source criticism, oral formulaic compositions, literary analysis and structuralism. But historical scholars coming to the study of Islam are surprised that no similar analysis or criticism has been applied by scholars to the history of Islam or the Koran. [87]

According to traditional accounts, the Koran was revealed to Mohammed, usually by an angel gradually over a period of years until his death in 632. Apparently nothing was written down, but the sura and verses were memorized and preserved by Mohammed's companions who heard his utterances. As we described previously, over 400 of these memorizers were killed at the Battle of Yamama in December 632, several months after Mohammed's death. The loss of such a large number of memorizers caused an enormous concern that much of the Koran would be irretrievably lost, and it motivated the first Caliph Abu Bakr and his successor Umar to appoint a committee to create a written collection suras and verses, based on the memories of the remaining memorizers. [92]

Zayd ibn Thabit (610-665), the former secretary of the Prophet, was selected to create this written manuscript. According to Zayd, he "started locating the Quranic material and collecting it from parchments, scapula, leafstalks of date palms and from the memories of men (who knew it by heart)." Zayd created the manuscript and then, several years later under orders from Caliph Uthman, Zayd updated his manuscript, making some corrections based on additional material from people who had known Mohammed decades earlier. Uthman made copies of the manuscript to be sent to other Muslim provinces, with orders that other Koran collections be destroyed. [88]

Therefore, there are two authoritative manuscripts in this story, both created by Zayd — the manuscript (around 634) ordered by Abu Bakr, and the updated manuscript (around 656) ordered by Uthman. Islamic clerics say that the updated manuscript still contains the precise utterances of Mohammed, as he spoke them decades earlier. [88]

Critical scholars point to massive holes in this story. The manuscripts were based on the testimonies of men who claim they heard it from Mohammed decades earlier. There was a bitterly vitriolic political atmosphere at that time (similar to the political atmosphere in America and Europe today), separating the friends of Abu Bakr (a Hashimite) from the friends of Uthman (an Umayyad). In particular, there was a bitter political battle between Uthman whose clan was to become the Sunnis, and Ali Ibn Abi Talib, the first Shia Imam. Recalling previous chapters when we discussed the selection of Caliphs, Uthman was considered by his political enemies to be guilty of nepotism and corruption, and to have been chosen as Caliph in an objectionable fashion. These enemies also objected to the methods used by Uthman to create the updated Koran manuscript. [87]

My own view, based on having observed politicians for my entire life, is that there is no possibility whatsoever that the Koran is a definitive collection of all unimpeachable utterances by Mohammed during his lifetime. The selection and interpretation of texts was controlled by a politician (Caliph Uthman) in a bitter political and ideological fight. Uthman was from the Umayya tribe, and his political opponent Ali Ibn Abi Talib was from Mohammed's Hashim tribe, and those two tribes had fought an extremely bloody civil war just 25 years earlier. These were all human beings, and the memories of atrocities by the other side would still exist, along with a desire for revenge.

Although some Muslim scholars claim that the Koran text is unimpeachable, there is nothing in my experience that leads me to believe that Uthman didn't filter all the texts according to his ideology, exclude some texts contrary to his ideology, and change a word here or there based on his ideology, and add other texts based on his ideology. The companions of Mohammed who had memorized the utterances were ordinary human beings with ordinary failing memories, and their testimonies could be easily changed under political pressure, possibly even under threat of torture (which is fairly common today).

Uthman ordered that all other versions of the Koran be destroyed, but some have survived, and there are different Korans used in some places. Muslim scholars in earlier centuries were flexible in conceding that parts of the Koran were lost or perverted, and that there were many thousand variants which made it impossible to talk of a unique Koran. [87]

Another issue is that the Koran was written in a defective script containing no vowels, and where even different forms of the consonants were indistinguishable from one another. In later centuries, there were disputes among scholars in different centers as to how consonants should be interpreted, and how vowels should be inserted. Even centuries later there were different versions of the Koran adopted by different regions — in Arabia, in Egypt, and in parts of Africa other than Egypt. [87]

According to one scholar, Charles Adams:

> "It is of some importance to call attention to a possible source of misunderstanding with regard to the variant readings of the Quran. The seven (versions) refer to actual written and oral text, to distinct versions of Quranic verses, whose differences, though they may not be great, are nonetheless substantial. Since the very existence of variant readings and versions of the Quran goes against the doctrinal position toward the Holy Book held by many modern Muslims, it is not uncommon in an apologetic context to hear the seven (versions) explained as modes of recitation; in fact the manner and technique of recitation are an entirely different matter."

Other scholars support the view that these orthographical variations lead to different interpretations. [87]

So we've described a number of issues in the developments of both the Bible and the Koran, and they're really quite similar, both riven with controversy. But there's one more thing that should be mentioned: The fact that these two books have survived and are still read every day by billions of people after almost two millennia proves how powerful and resilient both books are, and how they still affect the lives of people around the world.

Chapter 33. Violence in the Koran: The sword-verses

A major public debate today in the West is whether the Koran demands that all Muslims kill all non-Muslims, especially based on the so-called "sword-verses," which appear to command all Muslims to kill all non-Muslims. We wish to discuss this entire subject in detail, because of its importance today.

33.1. The empirical evidence — Muslim nations governed by Sharia law

Let's start with the empirical evidence. Empirical evidence is evidence obtained by observation or experience rather than just by theory. So, for example, if you have a complex theoretical "proof" from Quantum Mechanics that the sky is green, and then you look out the window and see that the sky is blue, then you have to discard your theoretical proof that the sky is green, since it's been disproven by empirical evidence that the sky really is blue.

So as to the question of whether all Muslims are commanded to kill all non-Muslims, we already have enormous amounts of empirical evidence that they are not.

One type of empirical evidence is that there are 90 Muslim-majority countries in the world today, all of them strict followers of Sharia law, and there are non-Muslims living in all of these countries, but they are not being killed. Furthermore this has been true throughout the 1400 years of Islam's existence. If the Koran or Sharia law demanded that non-Muslims be killed, then non-Muslims would be killed all the time in every country governed by Sharia law, and they are not.

33.2. The empirical evidence — Muslim wars of invasion

It's true that, in past centuries, Muslims have launched wars against Christians (e.g., the fall of Constantinople in 1453), but it's also true that Christians have launched wars against Muslims (e.g., the Crusades). There is no evidence that I'm aware of that the number of wars launched by Muslims and Christians is significantly greater for one than the other. Thus, the empirical evidence is that there is no significant difference between Muslims and Christians in the desire to kill each other.

33.3. The empirical evidence — Muslim populations involved in civil wars

It's true that there have been thousands of civil wars over the centuries, many involving Muslim populations, but I'm not aware of any evidence that Muslim populations are any better or worse than other populations.

Here are some of the major genocidal civil wars of the last century:

- Muslim Turks killed and displaced millions of Christian Armenians in 1915 during World War I.
- Orthodox Christian Josef Stalin ordered the starvation of millions of Orthodox Christian Ukrainians in 1931-35, in what has become known as the Holodomor.
- Officially atheist Mao Zedong committed a similar genocide of Chinese people in 1958-59, in what was called the Great Leap Forward.
- Christian Nazi Germany committed genocide against the Jews in the Holocaust in World War II in the 1940s.
- Buddhist leader Pol Pot lead a genocide against Buddhists in Cambodia in the "Killing Fields" civil war of 1975-79.
- Protestant Christian Robert Mugabe's ethnic Shona tribe committed genocide against the Nbdele tribe in Operation Gukurahundi in the early 1980s.
- Iraq's Sunni Muslim leader Saddam Hussein used chemical weapons against Sunni Muslim Kurds and Shia Muslim Iranians in 1987 in the Iran/Iraq war.

- Christian Hutus committed genocide of Christian Tutsis in the 1984 Rwanda genocide.
- Orthodox Christian Serbs committed the Srebrenica massacre of Bosnian Muslim men and boys in 1995 during the Bosnian war.
- Starting in 2004, white Muslims sponsored by the government of Sudan in Khartoum were slaughtering in large numbers the black Muslims in the western province of Darfur.
- Starting in 2012, Buddhists in Myanmar (Burma) have been committing genocide and ethnic cleansing against Muslim ethnic Rohingyas. This is continuing today.
- Starting in 2011, Syria's Shia/Alawite Muslim leader Bashar al-Assad, backed by Shia Muslim Iran, Shia Muslim Hezbollah, and Orthodox Christian Russia, have been committing genocide and ethnic cleansing against Sunni Muslims in Syria. This is continuing today.
- Starting in 2012, in Central African Republic, Muslim and Christian ethnic groups have been fighting a genocidal war against each other. This is continuing today.
- Starting in 2014 in Yemen, Sunni Muslims backed by Saudi Arabia and United Arab Emirates (UAE) have been fighting Iran-backed Shia Muslim Houthis. This is continuing today.

The above are only some of the major examples of genocidal civil wars in the last century, and they provide empirical evidence that there really isn't much difference between Muslims and people of other religions.

33.4. The empirical evidence — Extremist jihadists referencing Sharia law

Many people would claim that there is plenty of empirical evidence today that the Koran orders Muslims to kill non-Muslims, namely extremists jihadists claiming that it's their duty to kill the infidels. These jihadist groups include al-Qaeda (originally based in Afghanistan), the Taliban (originally based in Pakistan), the so-called Islamic State (IS or ISIS or ISIL or Daesh, originally based in Syria), al-Qaeda in the Arabian Peninsula (AQAP, based in Yemen), al-Qaeda in the Islamic Maghreb (AQIM), and numerous smaller groups. Each of the smaller groups usually declares allegiance to either al-Qaeda or ISIS, whether or not there's any actual communication between them.

I did some research on this in 2014, when some readers accused me of ignoring jihadist attacks on Christians. One person wrote (paraphrasing): "John, my point is that you left Christians off your list entirely, while at the same time they are being brutally massacred all around the world. You didn't get it then, perhaps due to your biases. You're not getting it now." Another person wrote, "Admit it. You don't like Christians and you downplay violence against them."

So after assuring readers that I wouldn't hesitate for a nanosecond to report on a massacre of Christians by jihadists or anyone else, I reported on some research to answer why don't I write about massacres of Christians more often. [105]

Let's look at some numbers. How many Christians have actually been massacred by jihadists? I went to the anti-Muslim "Religion of Peace" web site where they have tables of jihadist attacks, including a table of Christians killed by jihadists. Here are the numbers (as of 2014):

- Since 11-Sep-2001 (9/11) — that's 13 years — fewer than 9000 Christians have been killed in jihadist attacks, according to the web site.
- Since 1-Jan-2014 — that's this year alone — about 30,000 people have been killed in jihadist attacks.

A report sponsored by the BBC found that more than 5,000 people worldwide died in November alone — just one month — as a result of jihadist violence. This would indicate that about 60,000 people have died from jihadist attacks per year.

If you put all these figures together, you can see that the number of Christians killed by jihadists is minuscule — less than 2% --- compared to the total number of people killed by jihadists. Quite honestly, I would guess that in any given country in recent years, more Christians have been killed by traffic accidents than by terrorists. Overwhelmingly, the people being killed by jihadists are other Muslims.

So that explains the lack of media coverage of Christians killed by jihadists. If fewer than 2% of the victims are Christian, then you would expect Christians to get not much more than 2% of the coverage. [105]

So, the empirical evidence does not show that even extremist jihadist Muslims are targeting Christians, since they are responsible for only a minuscule number of Christian deaths compared to the number of Muslim deaths.

It's ironic that even extremist Sunni Muslim jihadists who are referencing the Koran to claim that "infidels must be killed" are almost always referring to other Muslims in other sects (Shias, etc.)

What we're actually seeing, based on empirical evidence, is something quite different from what is usually reported in the news, or claimed by ideologues on any side. If you put together everything we wrote above about wars in Sudan, Yemen, Syria and Burma, as well as the actions of extremist jihadists, is that it's Muslims, not Christians, who are being killed in massive numbers today. This is a remarkable situation that nobody talks about, and is profoundly significant for the world today. [105]

33.5. The 'Sword-Verses' of the Koran and the Jizya

Let's now look at the text of the two sword-verses, the verses that most people point to in order to "prove" that the Koran orders all Muslims to kill all non-Muslims:

> "Then, when the sacred months are drawn away, slay the idolaters wherever you find them, and take them, and confine them, and lie in wait for them at every place of ambush. But if they repent, and perform the prayer, and pay the alms, then let them go their way." (Koran 9:5)

and

> "Fight those who believe not in God and the Last Day, and do not forbid what God and His Messenger have forbidden – such men as practise not the religion of truth, being of those who have been given the Book – until they pay the tribute out of hand and have been humbled." (Koran 9:29)

The last sentence requires an additional explanation. It refers to what has become known as the "jizya," a special tax that Muslim governments impose on non-Muslims. Nominally, the purpose of the jizya is to pay for the government's protection of non-Muslims and their property from invaders. But in many cases, unscrupulous rulers used the jizya to oppress non-Muslims, or to increase their own private treasuries. [17]

33.6. Comparison of the Koran's sword-verses to the Bible's Old Testament

The sword-verses have been, at the very least, troubling to the defenders of Islam, and have been used by critics of Islam as proof that, as contrasted to Judaism and Christianity, Islam is a religion that commands its followers to kill non-believers, or "infidels."

There's a certain laughable, fairy tale aspect to this whole debate. Every major religion — Judaism, Christianity, Islam, Hinduism, Buddhism, and others — has a history full of wars of conquest, genocide and ethnic cleansing. In fact, they would not have become major religions if they were not, at the appropriate times in history, willing to slaughter, torture, rape, exterminate and commit other atrocities against "infidels." This is exactly how minor religions become major religions, and it's true of all major religions.

The Bible's Old Testament contains many examples where genocide and ethnic cleansing by the Jews was sanctioned or commanded by God. God commands the Israelites to seize the Land of Canaan and "dispossess all the inhabitants of the land." And in Deuteronomy 7:1–3, God commands the Israelites to wipe out all the Canaanites living in the Land of Israel: "You must doom them to complete destruction; grant them no terms and give them no quarter." Often God ensures military success for the Israelites, as in the war against the giant-king Og: "'Do not fear him, for I am delivering him and all his men and his country into your power' ... So the Lord our God also delivered into our power King Og of Bashan, with all his men, and we dealt them such a blow that no survivor was left" (Deut. 3:2–3). Dozens of other cases can be found throughout the remainder of the Bible, from the Book of Joshua to Second Chronicles. In modern times, the Nazi Holocaust triggered a major Jewish war of conquest, the war between Arabs and Jews in 1947 that followed the partitioning of Palestine and the creation of the state of Israel. [18]

And so the Bible, particularly the Old Testament, has its own "sword-verses" where God commands the Jews to commit genocide and ethnic cleansing.

However, those who criticize Islam say that there's a big difference between the "sword-verses" in the Bible and the Koran. The commandments to genocide and ethnic cleansing in the Old Testament, they say, are specific to certain battles at specific times in history, while the verses in the Koran are written in language that implies that they apply to all Muslims at all places and times and history. [16]

Those who support Islam specifically deny this claim, and say that sword-verses in the Koran are also restricted to a specific place and time, the Battle of Tabuk in October, 630 AD, Mohammed's final military battle before his death. It was apparently during the preparations for this battle that Mohammed uttered these verses.

Mohammed had achieved the conquest of Mecca in January, 630, after years of bloody ethnic civil war filled with, like all ethnic civil wars, slaughter, torture, and atrocities. Despite those atrocities, Mohammed granted clemency to the citizens of Mecca, in contradiction to the commandments of the sword-verses.

Later in the year, Mohammed received word that armies from the Christian Byzantine empire were approaching, with the intention of attacking Mohammed's Arab army. Mohammed raised an army and marched to Tabuk (Tabouk) to meet the Byzantines, but the information had been wrong, since there were no Byzantines to be met. [19]

It was during this march, apparently, that the sword-verses were uttered, and in this context they make perfect sense. After years of bloody, genocidal war, Mohammed's war-weary army was facing yet another battle with yet another enemy. Mohammed would have had to use as strong words as possible to motivate his army at that time. But it doesn't make sense to me that he would grant clemency to the non-believers in Mecca, and then say that all Muslims were commanded to kill all non-Muslims for all time.

This is a hotly debated question in the history of Islam, so you, Dear Reader, can make your own interpretation. But my own view, based on all the empirical evidence that I've presented, along with an analysis of the Battle of Tabuk, that the sword-verses were meant to apply specifically to the Battle of Tabuk, but not as a command to all Muslims to kill all non-Muslims at all places and times.

This is why I say that there is no such thing as Sharia law, in the sense of a fixed body of law. Empirically, Muslim governments have not seen the sword-verses as a command to kill non-Muslims. But extremist terrorist jihadists claim that's exactly what they mean. So Sharia law can be interpreted in any way that a leader or terrorist wants. So there's no such thing as Sharia law.

33.7. Comparisons of Jesus to Mohammed

People who compare Jesus to Mohammed usually don't take into account the times. Jesus's ministry was in a generational Awakening era, like America in the 1960s. Going into the temple and throwing over the tables of the money changers was a really 60s things to do, and something that 60s activist Abbie Hoffman might have done. During the 1960s, there were Christians who noted the same thing. The movie/play Jesus Christ Superstar, written in the 1960s, portrays Jesus as a 60s-style activist.

Mohammed's "ministry" occurred during a generational Crisis era, when there was a full scale war going on between two major clans in Mecca. Mohammed could not just do 60s-style activism, but had to be the general leading a full-scale generational crisis war. Both Jesus and Mohammed were men of their times, and their times were very different.

An interesting speculation is what Jesus would have been like if he had had to lead the Jews in war against the Romans. Instead, his followers had to have that war without him, 40 years after his death.

Chapter 34. Disputes over the authenticity of the Sunnah and Hadith

The Sunnah, literally meaning paths, methods or ways, are descriptions of the religious practices that were established by Mohammed among his companions, and passed on from generation to generation. These religious practices have mostly originated from the religion of Abraham, and Mohammed made revisions to them or some additions where appropriate. Although there are collections of Sunnah that do not strictly fit this definition, the "established" Sunnah are those practices based on the tradition of Abraham's religion which Mohammed established among his followers as religion, after reviving and modifying them if necessary. These practices were part of the every day life of the companions of Mohammed as the result of Mohammed establishing them among his companions. Then from the companions they were spread among all other people who accepted Islam at their time and then through them to the generations after. [89]

The Sunnah are derived from the consensus of generations. For example, celebrating Mohammed's birthday (Eid Milad) is not a Sunnah, because the consensus of generations have not recognized it as such, and that's because Mohammed himself did not establish it as an obligatory or recommended religious practice, and it emerged later in some Muslim communities. On the other had, celebration of the end of Ramadan, the month of fasting, on Eid al-Fitr is Sunnah because Mohammed established it as such, and it existed through a consensus of generations. [89]

There are thousands of Sunnah related to all aspects of life. Some examples are: [90]
- Show kindness to animals.
- When wearing clothes, start by the right side.
- Check inside shoes or socks before wearing them.
- Cool your meal before eating
- Food and drink should be taken with the right hand
- Clean your bed before sleeping
- Sleep on the right side
- Be efficient with water and don't waste

The Hadith are completely different. They are collections of testimonies of companions of Mohammed that narrate a story about Mohammed. Islamic clerics do not regard them as reliable as the Koran or the Sunnah, but they provide a rich source about Mohammed and how he lived, as well as the history of Islam and the Koran. [89]

There are hundreds of books of Hadith, with a total of hundreds of thousands of Hadith. Each Hadith is told in the form of a narration. Here are some examples:

Here's a hadith about prayer:

> "Narrated Abd Allah b. Shaqiq: I asked A'ishah [Mohammed's favorite wife] about the voluntary prayers offered by the Messenger of Allah. She replied: Before the noon prayer he would pray four rak'ahs [voluntary prayers] in my house, then go out and lead the people in prayer, then return to my house and pray two rak'ahs. He would lead the people in the sunset prayer, then return to my house and pray two rak'ahs. Then he would lead the people in the night prayer, and enter my house and pray two rak'ahs. He would pray nine rak'ahs during the night, including witr (prayer). At night he would pray for a long time standing and for a long time sitting. When he recited the Koran while standing, he would bow and prostrate himself from the standing position, and when he recited while sitting, he would bow and prostrate himself from the sitting position, and when dawn came he prayed two rak'ahs, then he would come out and lead the people in the dawn prayer."

A Hadith about marriage:

> "Narrated Abdullah ibn Abbas: A man came to the Prophet, and said: My wife does not prevent the hand of a man who touches her. He said: Divorce her. He then said: I am afraid my inner self may covet her. He said: Then enjoy her."

An eclipse of the sun occurred one day. Here is Mohammed's reaction, as described by his companion in a Hadith:

> "Narrated Abu Bakra: We were with Allah's Messenger when the sun eclipsed. Allah's Messenger stood up dragging his cloak till he entered the Mosque. He led us in a two-rak`at prayer till the sun (eclipse) had cleared. Then the Prophet said: The sun and the moon do not eclipse because of someone's death. So whenever you see these eclipses pray and invoke (Allah) till the eclipse is over." [91]

As we noted in the case of the Koran, the sura and verses were based on the utterances of Mohammed based on the fallible memories of fallible people, the people who had been companions of Mohammed in his lifetime, and even then the utterances were filtered by bitter political disputes between competing tribes.

In the case of the Hadith narrations, the situation is exponentially worse. These narrations are not the direct testimonies of companions of Mohammed, but they're the versions of these narrations that are passed down from one generation to the next, from father to son or mother to daughter, or teacher to student, and so forth. There are said to be six correct or authentic collections of traditions accepted by Sunni Muslims, namely, the compilations of Bukhari, Muslim, Ibn Maja, Abu Dawud, al-Tirmidhi, and al-Nisai. However, these collections were made many generations after the death of Mohammed. Bukhari died 238 years after the death of the Prophet, while al-Nisai died over 280 years after. [87]

Chapter 35. There's no such thing as Sharia law - again

Let's return to the subject of whether there's any such thing as Sharia law — in the sense of a fixed body of law adopted by all Muslims and all Muslim governments. We've shown the following:

- The principles of Sharia law vary widely from sect to sect, from country to country, and from era to era in the same country. We gave examples related to headscarves, killing infidels, and prayer styles, but we could have selected from thousands of examples showing the same concept.

- The Koran that we see today was created at the time of a bitter political battle between politicians from the Umayyad and Hashimite tribes, who had just fought a bloody civil war 25 years earlier and would become respectively the Sunni and Shia sects. The result there is that there is still some dispute about the authenticity of parts of the Koran.

- The Sunnah, religious practices adopted by Abraham and modified when necessary by Mohammed, are "established" by the consensus of generations. Although the "established" Sunnah are considered reasonably reliable, there are thousands of other Sunnah that have not been established.

- The Hadith, narrations of Mohammed's life provided by his companions, were not compiled until centuries later, and were filtered by multiple politicians. There are hundreds of thousands of Hadith, often contradicting each other, and mostly with very little or no authentication.

So, if you lead a country and want to adopt Sharia law, you can pick and choose pretty much anything you want. You start with a few core rules, like if you're Muslim then you have to pray five times a day, following one style or another — but even that rule would apply only to Muslims. Then you can select from thousands of Sunnah and hundreds of thousands of Hadith to make any rules you want. Just as in the case of Roman law, it's whatever you want.

In particular, if you're an extremist Sunni jihadist looking to slaughter, torture, rape, kill and commit other atrocities on Shia Muslims, then you can find some obscure Hadith narratives that you can misinterpret to support your view. That doesn't make you an esteemed Imam or Caliph; it means that you're a genocidal war criminal defiling and blackening Islam to support your horrific crimes.

When I say that there's no such thing as Sharia law, I mean that it's the same as Roman law — there's no fixed body of Sharia law, and it can be changed almost at will by politicians in different countries.

The widespread hysteria in the west with regard to Sharia law is based on ignorance and is totally unjustified. Just as there are good Jews and bad Jews, and good Christians and bad Christians, there are also good Muslims and bad Muslims, and Sharia law has nothing to do with it.

Chapter 36. Brief history of Catholic and Orthodox Christian 'Ecumenical' Councils

For the sake of comparison, we end this discussion of the Koran and Sharia (Islamic) law with a brief history of the development of Christian theology, and the numerous splits within Christian Churches. For this serious reader this serves two purposes. First, it describes several points of intersection between the developments of Islam and Christianity. And second, it allows comparison and contrast between how controversies and schisms are handled in the two religions.

36.1. The Ecumenical Councils

Christianity's first Ecumenical Council was held in 325 AD in Nicea, an ancient city just east of today's Istanbul (Constantinople). The Council of Nicea was a meeting of all Christian churches, led not by the Pope but by the Emperor Caesar Flavius Constantine of Rome. The objective of the meeting was to unify the different regional branches, and to resolve some important questions.

At that time, many questions of Christian theology had not yet been decided. One of the most important was the divinity of Jesus Christ. If Jesus was born, then how could he be divine? Although there was debate, the Council ratified the view that he was a man, but was God in the form of human flesh.

The details of how it makes sense that Jesus was both human and divine were extremely controversial. It was discussed further at the Second Ecumenical Council in Constantinople in 381, again in the Third Ecumenical Council, held in Ephesus, an Aegean sea port, in 431. By the time of the Fourth Ecumenical Council, held Chalcedon, near Constantinople, in 451, the differences on this issue were extremely vitriolic.

This was the time of the first major split within Christianity, as six branches of Christianity refused to recognize the Fourth Ecumenical Council, in a controversy that has never been resolved. Today, these are usually called the "Oriental Orthodox Christian" churches, comprised of the Ethiopian, Coptic (Egyptian), Armenian, Syrian, Indian and Eritrean Churches. These were all churches that had existed since apostolic times, and the major political issue was that they didn't wish to be controlled by Rome. The Fifth Ecumenical Council (in Constantinople in 553) and the Sixth Ecumenical Council (in Constantinople in 680) attempted without success to resolve the split.

36.2. The Seventh Ecumenical Council (787) - iconoclasts and iconophiles

The Seventh Ecumenical Council, in Nicea in 787, is the last one that was recognized. At this one, the major controversy was was between the "iconoclasts" and "iconophiles." "Iconoclast" means "image smasher" or destroyer of religious icons and monuments. The iconoclasts, who were outvoted, said that religious art was idolatry and must be destroyed. If Jesus is divine, is it not sacrilegious to worship an icon of Jesus as if it were Jesus himself? The iconophiles loved icons, and argued that they were man's dynamic way of expressing the divine through art and beauty. The latter argument won out.

The argument over icons was heavily influenced by the rise of Islam at that time. The Charlie Hebdo terror attack in Paris in January 2015 was supposedly motivated by prohibited artistic representations of the Prophet Mohammed, and this prohibition was coming into effect at the time of the Seventh Ecumenical Council.

36.3. The Catholic vs Orthodox Christian schism (1054)

That was the last time there was sufficient unity in the Christian churches to hold a worldwide Ecumenical Council, although there were smaller regional meetings.

In 1054, the Pope in Rome sent a letter to the Patriarch of Constantinople demanding that the latter submit to the Pope as head of all the churches. The Patriarch refused, and so the Pope and the Patriarch excommunicated each other on July 16, 1054. The "Schism of 1054" has never been healed.

Things got much worse in 1204 during the Crusades. The Catholics, on their way to fighting the Muslims in Jerusalem, sacked Constantinople, and placed a prostitute on the Emperor's throne at the church of St. Sophia. It was not until 2001 when the Pope John Paul visited Athens and, encountering large anti-Catholic protests, that the Catholics apologized for the sacking of Constantinople, and made a plea for forgiveness.

The Orthodox Christians were generally excluded from the Ecumenical Councils held by the Catholics over the centuries, but they were controversial nonetheless, even in modern times. The Second Vatican Council held by the Catholics in 1962-65 created a new split within the Catholic Church, when the Society of St. Pius X (SSPX) refused to recognize the legitimacy of its edicts. Pope Francis is currently working to heal this rift.

It was at the time of the Second Vatican Council that plans for an Ecumenical Council of all the Orthodox Churches was announced in 1961.

So in view of that history, it should not be surprising to anyone that the attempt to create a new Orthodox Christian Ecumenical Council, a Great and Holy Council (GHC) of Eastern Orthodox Churches, announced in 1961, has run into a great deal of controversy, as controversy has always been the norm, since the beginning.

36.4. Universal versus regional religions

It's the norm for religions to target small regional or national populations. You can be a "Catholic" anywhere in the world, but you can't just be an "Orthodox Christian." You have to be "Orthodox Christian" PLUS a nationality, such as a "Greek Orthodox" or a "Russian Orthodox" or some other branch.

The same thing is true of the Protestant religion, which has about 20 different churches in the United States alone, each targeting a different group.

In examining the history of religions, there are two conflicting phenomena. One is that a regional religion "becomes viral" and expands into a worldwide universal religion, and the other is that a universal religion splinters into regional religions.

In the case of Christianity, Judaism was a local religion that expanded into a more universal Christianity, and that splintered into the Catholic religion, which became truly universal, and regional Orthodox and Apostolic religions.

Islam has splintered into various sects, including Sunni Islam, Shia Islam, and smaller sects, such as the Zaydis, Alawites and Sufis. Only Sunni Islam has become truly universal.

The ancient Hindu religion has different sects and philosophies, but the caste system restricted the religion to India. There was a splintering in the form of Buddhism, which became a truly universal religion.

There are only three religions that have "gone viral" and become virtually universal: Catholicism, Sunni Islam and Buddhism. For example, in China, you'll find plenty of Catholics, plenty of Sunni Muslims, and plenty of Buddhists, but few Greek Orthodox or Shia Muslims or Hindus.

Chapter 37. Blasphemy and violence in Islam

37.1. Blasphemy laws in the UK and Ireland

Blasphemy laws are not unique to Islam. There have also been blasphemy laws in Christian countries, though most of them have been repealed in recent decades.

Blasphemy was a common law offence under Irish law when the 1937 Constitution explicitly made it an offence punishable by law, though it was seldom enforced. Several attempts to repeal the law have failed, and in 2009, a new Defamation Bill contained a clause saying, "A person who publishes or utters blasphemous matter shall be guilty of an offence and shall be liable upon conviction on indictment to a fine not exceeding 100,000 euros."

"Blasphemous matter" is defined as matter "that is grossly abusive or insulting in relation to matters held sacred by any religion, thereby causing outrage among a substantial number of the adherents of that religion; and he or she intends, by the publication of the matter concerned, to cause such outrage." However, prosecution of blasphemy in Ireland effectively ceased when the Church of Ireland was disestablished in 1869, though a man was prosecuted for burning of a Bible in 1885.

In Britain, prior to the 1900s, several people were flogged or imprisoned after being convicted of blasphemy. The last person in Britain to be sent to prison for blasphemy was John Gott, who in 1921 was convicted for publishing pamphlets satirizing the Bible, in which he compared Jesus to a circus clown. [23]

=inc ww2010.h4 xxx "Blasphemy laws in Pakistan"

It's well to remember that the Indian subcontinent, including what is currently Pakistan, was a British colony until 1947. And so blasphemy laws in Pakistan were at least partially inherited from Britain.

In Pakistan, in 1927, the British colonial rulers of the Indian subcontinent made it a criminal offence to commit "deliberate and malicious acts intended to outrage religious feelings of any class by insulting its religious belief". The law did not discriminate between religions.

As in the case of the UK and Ireland, the blasphemy law was rarely enforced. In the 58 years between 1927 and 1985, only ten blasphemy cases were heard in a court under this law. So in that sense, Pakistan's use of blasphemy law closely paralleled the use of blasphemy laws in the UK and Ireland.

However, things changed dramatically in the 1980s, with the rise of Generation-X, with its contempt that many members feel for their parents' generation. The public sphere was suddenly flooded with blasphemy charges, and 4,000 blasphemy cases have been heard since 1985.

In America in the 1980s, there was a similar development with false charges of rape. In the 1980s and early 1990s, feminists regularly charged men with false accusations of rape. Feminists particularly targeted black men, since they were the least able to defend themselves against false changes of rape, because of the claim that women never lied or were mistaken about rape. However, this use of false rape charges was abruptly ended in the 1990s because of a remarkable historic development — the use of DNA evidence in courtrooms to prove or disprove rape allegations. The Innocence Project, a non-profit organization, was able to reopen old rape cases and prove that the convicted rapist was innocent. Separately, tens of thousands of men accused of rape were able to prove their evidence using DNA evidence. Later research showed that 5-7% of rape accusations are fabricated by the accuser, and 25-30% of stranger rape victims identify the wrong person as the rapist. Although false charges of rape were sharply curtailed in the 1990s, the same phenomenon exists today in the form of the so-called "MeToo" movement, where a woman can accuse a man without evidence of having abused her or having "made her feel uncomfortable" years earlier, and have his career ruined. [73]

In Pakistan, there's no DNA test for false charges of blasphemy, and so these false charges have continued to this day. For example, Salman Taseer, the governor of the province of Punjab in Pakistan, was killed by his bodyguard Mumtaz Qadri in January 2015. Taseer had been advocating reform of the country's blasphemy laws, which had recently been used to sentence a Christian woman to death. A statement by 400 Pakistani religious scholars praised Qadri for keeping alive a "tradition of 1,400 years in Islam" which requires the killing of anyone committing an act of blasphemy against Prophet Mohammed. Qadri was showered with roses by Islamist lawyers when he arrived in court to face charges for murder. [24]

37.2. The 2015 Paris Charlie Hebdo terrorist attacks

In Pakistan today, it's possible to murder someone without punishment if you first charge him with blasphemy. However, this free use of blasphemy to excuse murder appears to be unique to Pakistan, and does not appear to be permitted in other Muslim countries.

However, a completely separate matter is jihadist terrorists. Statistics show that around 2% of people killed by jihadist terrorists are Christians, while hundreds of thousands of Muslims are being killed by other Muslims. Blasphemy, or "killing the infidels," is often used as an excuse for Muslims killing Muslims, as when Sunni jihadist terrorists commit mass murder in a Shia mosque.

Jihadist terrorist attacks on Christians are relatively rare by comparison, but when they occur, they often become worldwide news, and the jihadists use the charge of blasphemy as an excuse. On January 7, 2015, two masked gunmen, dressed in black and armed with Kalashnikov assault rifles, stormed the Paris offices of Charlie Hebdo magazine, opened fire and killed eight journalists, two police officers, a caretaker and a visitor. The stated reason for targeting Charlie Hebdo was that the magazine had committed blasphemy by publishing cartoons of Mohammed. They shouted, "We have avenged the prophet" and "Allahu akbar" (God is great). It's said to be the deadliest terror attack on French soil in 50 years, since 1961 when a right-wing paramilitary organization opposed to France's withdrawal from Algeria blew up a train killing 28 people. [22]

During the same week that the Charlie Hebdo attack occurred, Boko Haram terrorists in Nigeria in Africa killed 2000 people in a coordinated three-day rampage. Although 2000 people were killed, there was almost no news coverage, because all worldwide news coverage was completely taken over by the deaths of the 12 people in the Charlie Hebdo attack. [108]

37.3. Iran's death fatwa against Salman Rushdie and 'Satanic Verses'

On February 14, 1989, Iran's leader Ruhollah Khomeini issued a death sentence fatwa targeting author Salman Rushdie, claiming that his novel *Satanic Verses* was a blasphemous attack on Islam. The fatwa read: [20]

"I inform the proud Muslim people of the world that the author of the Satanic Verses book, which is against Islam, the Prophet and the Koran, and all those involved in its publication who are aware of its content are sentenced to death."

Rushdie denied that his novel was blasphemous, but to no avail. As we've seen in more recent examples, particularly in Pakistan, if you want to murder someone and not be punished, then first charge him with blasphemy to Islam, based on flimsy evidence or no evidence.

For many years, Rushdie had police protection from the UK government. He is still alive in 2018.

In 2016, hardline Iranian news media outlets have raised an additional $600,000 to add to the reward for killing Rushdie under the fatwa. According to an Iranian senior editor: "The fatwa against Salman Rushdie is a religious fatwa. Nobody in the world can nullify a religious fatwa. It has been, it is, and it will be." [21]

As we'll describe later in this book, in conjunction with Khomenei's constitution, which forces the government to be corrupt, Iran's government is one of the most corrupt in the world. So it seems likely that the entire Rushdie fatwa is less a religious fatwa and more a corrupt fundraising fatwa.

Part VIII. Shia Islam Theology

Chapter 38. The twelve infallible Imams

38.1. The Sunni-Shia theological split

In the decades following Mohammed's death, there were conflicts as to who would succeed Mohammed as caliph of Islam. One group insisted that any new caliph must be a direct descendant of Mohammed's family.

Ali Ibn Abi Talib (601-661), known simply as Ali, was the husband of Mohammed's daughter, and was therefore the son-in-law of Mohammed, as well as Mohammed's close companion. Ali was Mohammed's first choice to be the successor to him as Caliph, but as we described in earlier chapters, Ali only became Caliph years later in 656, after Uthman was assassinated.

When Ali was assassinated in 661, his brother al-Husayn ibn Ali became leader of the Shias. The relationship between Mohammed's Hashimite clan versus its bitter enemies the Umayyad clan continued and worsened.

Al-Husayn was killed in the seminal Battle of Karbala in a generational crisis war that climaxed in 680, splitting the Muslim community, and throwing the question of succession into chaos. In the following decades, the group that won the war (the Umayyads) became known as the Sunnis, and they selected caliphs by a variety of means, including elections, inheritance, and wars.

The Shias formed a completely separate branch of succession, referring to their leaders as Imams. They continued to insist that any imam must be a descendant of Mohammed, and must therefore be a direct descendant of al-Husayn ibn Ali. As it turned out, al-Husayn had nine descendants, with the last one, the 12th imam, disappearing in 873.

38.2. Fivers, Seveners and Twelvers

Today, Shia Muslims are still divided over which of these imams was going to return as the messiah to avenge injustices to the Shia. This belief is roughly equivalent to the Christian belief in the second coming of Christ, or the Buddhist belief in the Maitreya — that a new Buddha is to appear on earth, and will achieve complete enlightenment.

One Shia sect broke off in 740 and were known as the Zaydis, or "Fivers," because of their allegiance to the fifth imam. These are the Houthis today. They took hold in southern Arabia (currently Yemen) in the century following the death of the prophet Mohammed.

Another Shia sect are called "Seveners," because of their allegiance to the seventh imam. Some Hazaras in Afghanistan are Ismaili Shia, also known as Seveners. [31]

Most Shias today are "Twelvers," because of their allegiance to the 12th imam, also called "The Hidden Imam," who disappeared in 873, as described above. According to the Twelver belief, he did not die, but disappeared and became "hidden," and will reappear at the appropriate time.

Chapter 39. The disappearance of al-Mahdi and the rise of the Shia jurists

39.1. The Occultation — the disappearance of the 12th Imam (940 AD)

By the tenth century, mainstream Shia theology had settled on the belief that there had been 12 infallible Imams, all of them descendants of Mohammed. This theology was the direct result of the disappearance of Imam Muhammad Al-Mahdi in 940 AD. As this was the last descendant of Mohammed, there was no 13th Imam to succeed him, and so, according to Shia theology, an "occultation" occurred in 940 — al-Mahdi is still alive, but in hiding.

As an aside, the Shia belief is that the occultation had two parts. The minor occultation began in 874, when the Imam was hidden, but communicated with the world through his deputies. The major occultation occurred in 940, when the last of the deputies died, and there was no further contact with Imam al-Mahdi. [62]

It's actually amazing how the disappearance of al-Mahdi over a millennium ago has had such an enormous effect on Shia Islam and Iran today. In a way it's not surprising. The crucifixion of Jesus Christ two millennia ago has an enormous effect on the Christianity religion today, as it should, so it's quite reasonable to discover that the disappearance of al-Mahdi has an enormous effect on the Shia Islam religion today.

But that's religion, not politics. The difference in the disappearance of al-Mahdi is the enormous influence it has on the politics of Iran today. In fact, the entire history of Iran since then has been a controlling factor in the politics of Iran, as well as the religion of Shia Islam in Iran. Indeed, the possible return of al-Mahdi as the messiah to avenge injustices to the Shia Muslim believers is a dominant feature of Iran's politics today.

The disappearance of al-Mahdi created a huge problem for Iran. The twelve infallible Imams had been both religious and political leaders, but particularly they were the only legitimate political leaders of the Shia community. When al-Mahdi disappeared, there was no longer a legitimate political leader, and no way for the Shias in Iran to produce one, except to sit back and wait for al-Mahdi to return. This lack of political leadership itself performed a political function because it became prudent, almost always living as minorities in Sunni societies, to stay aloof from politics. [10]

39.2. The rise of Shia jurists and Shia jurisprudence

Well, this is obviously a big problem, since any society or country needs a political leader to do things like declare war, collect taxes, and settle mundane disputes. So the Shias need to come up with way of doing the things that a political leader would normally do.

The method used was fascinating. There was no political leader, but there were the usual jurists, or judges. There was also a problem solving system which, combined with the jurists, provided the functions of the political leader. Because the system was guided by a strict set of rules, we can almost compare it to the jurists following a computer algorithm.

The problem solving system algorithm receives inputs (questions) and creates outputs (answers). The four components of this system are the Koran, the Sunnah, Aql (Reason), and Ijma (Consensus). This means that when a jurist is confronted with a question, he uses his reason to interpret the Koran and Sunnah and answer the question. A jurist will compare his answer with past and present jurists to reach a consensus on the best answer if possible. Political questions that would normally be answered by a political leader would be answered by jurists applying this problem solving system to political questions. [10]

The historical role of Shia jurists in Iran until the modern era was twofold: Qaza (judicial) and Ifta (issuing religious commandments or fatwa). This means that the jurist was tasked with acting as a judge in legal disputes using Sharia (Islamic law) and issuing fatwas based on questions asked of them. These fatwas were limited to answering questions involving purely local disputes, and so jurists stayed out of politics. [10]

39.3. Sheikh Morteza Ansari and the Tobacco Revolt

As we've discussed in earlier chapters, the 1800s was a time when nations were formed and wars were held to try to settle boundaries.

Iran was heavily involved in its own nation-building, and so a political leader was increasingly needed. But the Shia Muslim community had managed centuries earlier to box itself into a corner by declaring that all political systems were illegitimate and participation in them was prohibited, until the return of al-Mahdi.

Sheikh Morteza Ansari (1781–1864) developed a new theory of Shia jurisprudence that sought to get around these problems. For centuries, the jurists had issued fatwas on an ad-hoc basis to resolve local disputes, but not large political issues. Ansari theorized that fatwas could be used to fight injustice in politics, by using them in a systematic way to place a religious straightjacket on and thereby pressure political authorities. Thus, while formally rejecting a political role for Shia jurists, he revolutionized Shia jurisprudence by opening the path for their intervention in politics through fatwas. [10]

Ansari's Shia political jurisprudence was only theoretical at the time he developed it, but it was put into practice by his disciples. Recall from our previous discussion of the Tobacco Revolt (1890) that it was an anti-government protest launched by merchants, and put into effect by a fatwa issued by a cleric, Mirza Mohammed Hassan Husseini Shirazi (1814-1896). The text of that fatwa was as follows:

> "In the name of God the Merciful, the Forgiving. Today the use of tunbaku and tobacco, in whatever fashion, is reckoned as war against the Imam of the Age (may God hasten his glad advent)" [42]

The "Imam of the Age" is, of course, al-Mahdi. This fatwa went far beyond the usual role of settling a local dispute. Following Ansari's theory of Shia political jurisprudence, jurist Shirazi's fatwa enjoined the entire Shia community from using tobacco as a violation of Sharia law, and thereby pressured the Shah to withdraw the tobacco concession. Shirazi's practical application of Ansari's theory began to normalize the notion that jurists had a role to play in politics. [10]

39.4. Shia jurisprudence and the Constitutional Revolution

We wrote about the Constitutional Revolution (1905-09) earlier in this book as bloody crisis civil war. It began as a popular political movement to replace the dictatorship of a Shah with unlimited powers with a constitutional form of government, with checks and balances, to limit the power of the Shah, and strengthen the other branches of government, the Majlis (parliament) and the judiciary.

In parallel with the political developments and the war, there was also a struggle among the jurists in the clergy to take advantage of the Constitutional Revolution for their own benefit. Just as there were two sides in the civil war, pro- and anti-constitution, killing each other, there were also two sides among the jurists.

However, the jurists were operating under the handicap that, until the return of al-Mahdi, there could be no such thing as a legitimate political system. But in the 1800s Iran changed from a collection of tribes into a nation-state, and so by the beginning of the 1900s a political system was required. So for the clergy, all they could choose from would be options within an illegitimate political system. During the Constitutional Revolution, the two major options would be an illegitimate government with or without a constitution.

The pro-constitution group argument that when choosing between an unaccountable tyrannical system and an accountable constitutional one, the latter was the lesser of two evils. A system based on the whims of an individual had the potential to do more harm to the Shia than one based on the popular will as expressed in the popularly elected Majlis (parliament). However, it was necessary to prevent populist movements that violated Sharia law. Therefore, the Shia jurists would participate in this system by being present in parliament and its deliberations to prevent violations of Sharia law. [10]

The second group opposed constitutionality because they believed the popular will could be more dangerous to Islam than a despotic government. Constitutionality could only be less harmful to the Shia if its laws and policies adhered to Sharia law as interpreted by jurists. This led to a demand that jurist must do more than participate in the parliament's deliberations — they must actually lead parliament and have a veto over its decisions. [10]

The synthesis of these two opposing views was that whatever illegitimate political system was in place, it had to be guided by Shia jurists, not by popular will. There might be elected politicians in the government, but one way or another the Shia jurists had to have some level of control, to prevent popular will from violating Sharia law.

The outcome was quite amazing. By the conclusion of the Constitutional Revolution, the concepts of the constitution and the majlis had survived and been accepted, but in a form acceptable to the Shia jurists: Jurists would preside over their historical domain of the judiciary, influence politics through fatwas, and, most remarkably, would take executive and legislative authority through control of parliament.

There was still a constitutional role for popular will, but it would be subordinated, to a lesser or greater extent, by the Shia jurists enforcing their views on Sharia law. Theoretical there were three branches of government, but practically there would be only one — political control by the Shia jurists. [10]

39.5. Theory of Wilayat al-Faqih (Guardianship of the Jurist)

Recall that Ayatollah Ruhollah Khomeini had led the anti-government protests in the 1963 White Revolution. His followers were tortured, jailed and killed, and Khomeini himself was exiled. In earlier chapters, I described the political history of how the White Revolution led to the 1979 civil war (Islamic Revolution).

Now we turn to the religious underpinnings of this political transition. Since Shia Islam, in the absence of al-Mahdi, considers all political systems to be illegimate, how did Khomeini find a way to justify as legitimate the political system that he set up in 1979? Khomeini's contribution to Shia theology was to find a way to create a legitimate political system that would have been considered illegitimate by Shia clerics for the previous millennium.

Khomeini's radical conclusion was to completely reject the notion that a Shia nation could not have a legitimate political system. He reasoned that God would not have abandoned the Shia Muslims in this way, and that the problem therefore was to formulate a kind of political system that would work as well as the political systems led by the 12 infallible Imams of ancient times. [10]

Khomeini's solution is to create the office of "Guardian Jurist," filled by a person (himself) with essentially dictatorial power. He can set the general guidelines for the political system, supervise policy implementation, and exert profound influence over the three branches of government. As commander-in-chief, he can declare war and peace, mobilize the armed forces, and appoint their commanders. No prominent previous Shia theology had ever conceived of jurists wielding such immense power in the manner articulated by Khomeini. [10]

Khomeini's solution foresaw a Guardian Jurist who, like the original nine infallible Imams, would be divinely guided, and therefore would have the power to make all decisions. Khomeini's concept did not contain any place for popular will or democracy. However, Khomeini was leading a revolution that was demanding a democracy in place of the dictatorship of the Shah. In fact, 70 years after the Constitutional Revolution, the followers of Khomeini's revolution were demanding a constitutional democracy.

To resolve this conundrum, Khomeini had to find a way to set up a dictatorship which was also a democracy. This isn't as hard as it seems, since dictators rig elections in countries around the world on a daily basis. But for Khomeini, this kind of dictatorial control had to be embedded within a constitution that was nominally democratic.

Khomeini might have been influenced by the dictatorial system in the Soviet Union, which was considered very fashionable and stylish in the among the left hoi polloi in the 1970s, before the Soviet Union crashed and burned in the 1980s. In the Soviet system in the 1970s, there was a Politburo, with absolute power. It had 14 members, with a top member, the General Secretary, who always had the crucial vote on key issues. According to the regulations, the Politburo was elected from below - by the delegates of the Communist Party Congresses - every 4-5 years. This is how the Soviets managed to have a dictatorship, with a veneer of democracy. [13]

If Khomeini was aware of and influenced by the Soviet Politburo system, then he would also have seen its disadvantages. Although the Communist Party Congresses were tightly controlled, there might still be some sort of populist revolt that could unseat the preferred members of the Politburo. Even worse, the people in the Politburo could switch their allegiance to other groups and leaders. This in fact happened to Nikita Khrushchev, who became General (First) Secretary in 1957, but was forced out in 1964 when influential party leaders decided to replace him with Leonid Brezhnev. Brezhnev was in power until 1979, when his health began to deteriorate, but he held onto power until his death in 1982. [13]

Khomeini had to resolve the contradiction between the immense power of the Guardian Jurist versus the popular will and democratic elections. He may have used the highly fashionable Politburo example as a starting point, but his structure was much more complex and made it much more certain that the Guardian Jurist could not be removed, even though it still had elements of democracy.

So, the Guardian Jurist is supreme over the state, but he is appointed by the Assembly of Experts. The Assembly of Experts for the Leadership is an 88-member body of Islamic jurists, elected by direct popular vote every eight years. According to the Constitution, the Assembly's mandate is to appoint, monitor, and dismiss (if appropriate) the Supreme Leader. In practice, the Assembly has never really questioned the supreme leader. [14]

Although the Assembly of Experts is elected by a popular vote, few people qualify to run. Candidates for the Assembly must be masters of Islamic jurisprudence, pass several written and oral exams, and finally must be approved by the Guardians Council, which oversees the entire election, and decides who is eligible to run. [15]

Next, the Guardian Council is a powerful 12-member council with vast legislative and executive powers. It consists of twelve members, six of whom are theologians who are appointed by the Guardian Jurist (the Supreme Leader), and six who are jurists, versed in different legal branches, appointed by the parliament (Majles) from among the "Muslim jurists" specified by the head of the judicial system. And who appoints the head of the Judicial System? The Guardian Jurist (Supreme Leader). [15]

So, to summarize, the Guardian Jurist is selected by the "democratically elected" Assembly of Experts. Only people approved by the Guardians Council are eligible to run for the Assembly of Experts. Half of the Guardians Council is appointed by the Guardian Jurist. The other half are appointed from the parliament — but selected from a list of "Muslim jurists" specified by the head of the judicial system — who is appointed by the Guardian Jurist.

Comparing Khomeini's Guardianship of the Jurist system to the Soviet Politburo, we can see that even though both of them in theory are democracies, Khomeini's system gives him much more control as dictator then the Soviet General Secretary has. Khomeini's system also has the advantage that it's far too complex for the ordinary Iranian to understand it, allowing the Supreme Leader and other politicians to easily obfuscate what's going on.

Part IX. Shia theology in practice under Khomeini

Chapter 40. Wilayat al-Faqih in practice

40.1. Divine guidance vs popular will

Shia theological theory has been confounded for more than a millennium by the disappearance of the "12th Infallible Imam," Imam Muhammad Al-Mahdi in 940 AD. The 12 Imams are seen as being successors of Mohammed himself — as infallible political leaders, representing the highest level of piety, and embodying the same qualities as exemplified by Mohammed himself. [12]

Without an infallible Imam to serve as leader, there could be no political leader at all, since no ordinary human being could be as infallible as the 12 infallible Imams. Khomeini's theory of Wilayat al-Faqih provides a means for selecting someone who is as close to infallible as possible, a just and capable jurist to serve as a leader in the place of an actual infallible Imam.

It would be an exaggeration to say that Wilayat al-Faqih was "dead on arrival," but it would not be wrong to say that, being administered by non-infallible humans looking for money and power, the doctrine was manipulated to whatever extent desired to meet any sort of political goal.

The theological doctrine itself began with a fatal flaw: it didn't resolve the conflict between divine guidance and popular will. As a practical matter, any society contains a substantial minority of people who are not religious, and do not believe in divine guidance. So if the Supreme Leader is selected by some sort of democratic process, then he derives his legitimacy from the democratic process and the will of the people. Even in Khomeini's complex selection scheme, the Supreme Leader is chosen by the Assembly of Experts who are, in turn, selected in a democratic process, and who are empowered to supervise and remove the Supreme Leader. But in Iran, the Assembly of Experts have been unable to exercise their supervisory duties, based on the argument that, in fact, popular will is irrelevant, and the Supreme Leader is divinely guided, just like the infallible Imams. To a lot of the public, this is not sufficient. [10]

Ayatollah Rouhollah Khomeini, the first Supreme Leader of the Islamic Republic, assumed that, in a rightly ordered state, God's will (as determined by the clerics) and the people's will (as manifested through elections) would coincide. This happened during the first years of the generational Recovery era following the civil war. But as young people with no personal memories of the war entered their teen years, anti-government protests began, and had to be violently put down by bloody massacres.

Events quickly showed that the hardline government of Iran was as bad as, or worse than, the government of the Shah that had been replaced. There was Khomenei's bloody revenge massacre in 1988, the student anti-government protests in 1999, the anti-government protests in the 2009 elections, and many others. At the very least, this proved Khomeini and Khamenei were not by any means legitimized by popular will, and are less and less legitimized as younger generations come of age.

This means that they're justifying their violence by "divine guidance." Apparently Allah is telling the Supreme Leader and the Islamic Revolutionary Guard Corps (IRGC) that it's a good idea to torture, rape and kill peaceful protesters, including innocent women and children.

40.2. The third way: Corruption

Khomenei's theology today is in shambles. If the Supreme Leader is not deriving his legitimacy from either divine guidance or the will of the people, then what's left? There's a third way, used by violent dictators for millennia: corruption.

According to Transparency International, Iran's government is among the most corrupt in the world. According to its transparency index, Iran has an extremely low score of 30 out of 100, ranked at 130 out of 180. By comparison, the worst performing region in the world is sub-Saharan Africa, with a score of 32, which is a better score than Iran's. [98]

Corruption was considered so endemic and universal in 1978, that it was a major factor in the anti-government riots against the Shah that occurred at that time, according to a Washington Post article on November 19, 1978:

"Flushed by billions of dollars from oil revenues and other development projects, corruption has become so universal, ordinary Iranians complain, that the corner grocer jacks up prices, off government inspectors had passes the added costs on to the customers.

A foreign banker said the growing blatancy of corruption was on a mammoth scale. "In one deal I know of," he said, "eight people received bribes involving sums which I would not make for several years."

As a result corruption has become the target for the torrent of demonstrations against the shah. As an indication of the growing public pressure, two investigative bodies were set up during the past 10 days. They bring the total to at least four separate agencies that have been established to delve into alleged wrongdoing by civil servants, wheelers and dealers, the royal family and the Pahlavi Foundation, an investment fund which controls a portion of the shah's riches for the benefit of the poor....

Public cynicism is based on the deeply embedded notion that the shah has used corruption as a system of government to buy loyalty and that the Pahlavi Foundation long has served as a tax-free slush fund for the royal family rather than for charity as it is advertised."

That "torrent of demonstrations against the shah" led to Khomeini's Great Islamic Revolution the following year.

40.3. The missing checks and balances

For millennia, philosophers and politicians have understood that the greatest threats to any form of government are corruption and despotism. Even before the advent of constitutions, there were laws and conventions that implemented "checks and balances" designed to prevent these evils.

There are two kinds of "separation" laws that have been tried:

- Separation of Church and State (separation of religion and government). In theory, this can provide a way to control corruption by allowing the Church and the State to check each other, although it's probably more common for religious and government institutions to join in corruption for their common benefit. Within Christianity, Western Christian (Catholic and Protestant) states have typically implemented this separation, while Eastern Christian states have typically incorporated religion into the national identity (Greek Orthodox Church, Russian Orthodox Church, etc.). In this sense, Muslim states are similar to Eastern Christian states.

- Separation of Powers. The regime of ancient Rome was described as having three branches: monarchy (the consul, or chief magistrate), aristocracy (the Senate) and democracy (the people). There were many variations of this over the centuries, and it was fully incorporated into the United States Constitution, with an Executive, a Congress and a Judicial branch. [96]

With regard to the United States government, the separation of powers implements checks and balances throughout the government. In order to contrast this to Iran's government, here are examples of checks and balances in the US government: [96]

- The president (head of the executive branch) serves as commander in chief of the military forces, but Congress (legislative branch) appropriates funds for the military and votes to declare war. In addition, the Senate must ratify any peace treaties.
- Congress has the power of the purse, as it controls the money used to fund any executive actions.
- The president nominates federal officials, but the Senate confirms those nominations.
- Within the legislative branch, each house of Congress serves as a check on possible abuses of power by the other. Both the House of Representatives and the Senate have to pass a bill in the same form for it to become law.
- Once Congress has passed a bill, the president has the power to veto that bill. In turn, Congress can override a regular presidential veto by a two-thirds vote of both houses.
- The Supreme Court and other federal courts (judicial branch) can declare laws or presidential actions unconstitutional, in a process known as judicial review.
- In turn, the president checks the judiciary through the power of appointment, which can be used to change the direction of the federal courts
- By passing amendments to the Constitution, Congress can effectively check the decisions of the Supreme Court.

- Congress (considered the branch of government closest to the people) can impeach both members of the executive and judicial branches. [96]

Now looking at the constitution that Khomeini, we see almost none of these checks and balances, and indeed Khomeini didn't see the need for any. He created the office of "Guardian Jurist" to be filled by a person who was almost as infallible as the 12 infallible Imams. In doing so, he made the Guardian Jurist a virtual dictator. It's true that the Assembly of Experts theoretically supervises the Guardian Jurist, but the powers are so weak as to be nonexistent. This is proven by the fact that in 40 years the Assembly of Experts has never reversed a decision of the Supreme Leader.

40.4. The Principlists versus the Reformists

The politicians in Iran are generally in three major categories:
- The Principlists, mostly consisting of survivors of the 1979 Great Islamic Revolution, are the most hardline, demanding that society continue to adhere to the "principles" set by the 1979 Revolution. The Principlists will claim that the Supreme Leader is as infallible as the 12 infallible Imams, even when he's ordering the slaughter, rape and torture of innocent college students.
- The Pragmatics or Moderates are mostly in the same generation as the Principlists, and adhere to Principlist concepts, but wish to institute some reforms that would recognize popular will (as opposed to divine guidance). They also advocate a closer relationship with the West.
- The Reformists, mostly consisting of younger generations that have grown up after the 1979 Revolution, are still "conservative" by Western standards, but are demanding reforms of the hardline rules, including deep political reforms and even regime change. They typically fight for the same issues as American Boomers in the 1960s — greater freedom in gender issues, greater freedom of speech and protest, and reluctance to engage in foreign wars, such as the war in Syria.

Chapter 41. The Future of Iran

41.1. December 2017 protests - challenge to Supreme Leader's legitimacy

Iran's president Hassan Rouhani in 2015 had promised the Iranian people that the economy would improve significantly after Iran reached the nuclear deal with America and the West, because of the removal of economic sanctions. By December 2017, unemployment stood at 12.4%, up 1.4% from previous year, while prices and inflation were surging, and it was clear that the economy had only gotten worse since the signing of the nuclear deal. The perception among the Iranian people was that Rouhani and Iran's government had received tens of billions of dollars from the removal of sanctions, but that the money had been wasted on government corruption and foreign wars.

The results was widespread demonstrations in cities across Iran, and the usual government crackdown on peaceful protesters. An anti-government organization advocating for the removal of Iran's hard-line regime, the People's Mojahedin Organization of Iran (PMOI / MEK), collected a list of the slogans being chanted by protesters in different cities. Some of them are listed below. [107]

The original protests were about the economy and government corruption:

- Bread, work, freedom
- The nation is destitute while the leader is acting like God
- Young people are unemployed, and mullahs have all the positions
- Execute the economically corrupt
- If you stop one case of embezzlement, our problem will be solved

Within two days, they had morphed into general anti-government and anti-regime protests:

- Seyed Ali [Khamenei] shame on you let go of our country
- Dignified Iranians, join your people
- We don't want an Islamic Republic
- Dignified Iranians, support us, support us
- Death to the Dictator

- Death to Rouhani
- Don't be afraid, we are all united
- Political prisoners should be freed
- Shame on you
- Death or freedom

Anti-war protests zeroed in on Iran's enormous expenditures on war efforts for Syria, Iraq, Lebanon, Hezbollah, Hamas, and Yemen:

- Leave Syria, think about us
- Guns and tanks! The mullahs must be killed
- Death to Hezbollah
- Leave Syria alone, think about us instead
- Forget about Gaza and Lebanon; I'll sacrifice my life for Iran
- Never mind Palestine, think about us [107]

Gholam Ali Jafarzadeh Emenabadi, a member of Iran's parliament, said that Iran's Constitution is unable to counter corruption, and says that corruption in Iran has to begin with the Supreme Leader:

"If the revolution faces problems, we should know that this is caused by widespread corruption.

It is advisable to start fighting corruption in the office of the spiritual leader, and I think if this happens then we will fight corruption in the Judiciary, and then the executive power (the government) will begin to cleanse itself of corruption." [99]

In fact, an April 2017 study by Gan anti-corruption portal found massive corruption at all levels of Iran's government:

"Companies operating or planning to invest in Iran face a very high risk of corruption. A powerful system of political patronage, nepotism and cronyism pervade all sectors of the economy. Irregular payments and bribes are often exchanged to obtain services, permits or public contracts. The Rouhani government has addressed the need to curtail corruption but fails to exert enough pressure on hardliners in control of key state institutions, including the Islamic Revolutionary Guards Corps (IRGC) and the judiciary. While there are multiple laws in place that criminalize various forms of corruption in both the public and private sectors, they are not effectively enforced in practice and impunity is pervasive." [100]

According to the report, the judicial system, the police, the public services, land administration, tax administration, customs administration, public procurement, natural resources, and the repressive civil society are all rife with bribery, kickbacks, and other corruption. Even reporting corruption is met with harsh penalties and jail. Freedoms of assembly and association are also strongly limited, with harsh penalties. Human rights activists are routinely arrested without formal charges and sometimes without access to legal counsel. [100]

41.2. Replacing the Constitution

It's widely understood, both inside and outside Iran, that Iran's government is among the most corrupt in the world. There are frequent calls from the Moderates and Reformists to take steps to eliminate corruption, but unfortunately that's impossible. As we've just discussed, Iran's constitution contains no checks and balances of the kind that the US constitution is full of. To the contrary, Iran's constitution was specifically set up by Khomeini to give him as much power as possible, since he viewed himself delusionally to be as infallible as the Infallible Imams.

The US constitution was created by a completely different process. The first constitution, the Articles of Confederation, was agreed in 1781, when the Revolutionary War was still in progress, at a time when the nation was a loose confederation of states, each operating like independent countries. The Articles of Confederation gave Congress the power to govern foreign affairs, conduct war and regulate currency, but had no power to enforce its decisions.

After the war ended, it was clear that the Articles of Conferation had to be replaced. A Constitutional Convention opened in 1787. Reporters and other visitors were barred from the convention sessions, which were held in secret to avoid outside pressures.

The lesson to be learned here is that creating a more perfect Constitution is a process. Corruption is so bad that Iran's Assembly of Experts could call for an Iranian constitutional convention, charged with creating a new constitution based on the lessons learned from Khomeini's constitution. The current Supreme Leader, who is aging and ill, might well support this process, provided that it's framed so that he gets the credit and preserves his legacy.

The British historian Lord Acton wrote the following in 1887: "Power tends to corrupt, and absolute power corrupts absolutely. Great men are almost always bad men." In 40 years, this has proven to be the case in the Islamic Republic of Iran. This will not change in Iran unless the Constitution is replaced.

41.3. Selecting a successor to Supreme Leader Khamenei

The current Supreme Leader, Seyed Ali Khamenei, was born in 1939 and has been Supreme Leader since 1989. Like many strongman dictators in the world, Khamenei might be in office until his age is in the 90s. However, there are rumors that Khamenei is seriously ill, and there is a great deal of talk, both inside and outside of Iran, that Khamenei will soon have to be replaced.

Selim Celal, a Turkish foreign policy analyst has provided four possible scenarios for the selection of Khamenei's successor: [97]

- Removal of the Supreme Leader, and an end to the theocratic government.
- Replace the Supreme Leader with a Supreme Leadership Council. This option was actually considered when Khomeini died.
- Succession by an Ayatollah, just as Khamenei replaced Khomeini in 1989.
- Succession by Khamenei's son, Mojtaba Khamenei.

Each of these scenarios, and others as well, has its political supporters and enemies. Each of these scenarios will mean wealth and power for some current political leaders, and will mean devastation, jailing or execution for others.

The important question for Iran is not who is going to succeed Khamenei, but how is the problem that Iran is among the most corrupt nations in the world going to be resolved. As we've discussed in preceding sections, the current constitution promotes and dictates corruption, since it contains no checks and balances and gives the Supreme Leader almost absolute power. Thus, resolving the corruption problem requires replacing the constitution.

Of the four scenarios listed above, the last two would require a minor change to the Constitution or no change at all, while the first two would require a major change or rewrite.

I think it's important to make clear what I'm saying here. I'm not saying that it would ideological preferable or nice for Iran to replace its constitution. I'm saying that Iran is almost mathematically forced to be one of the most corrupt nations in the world under the current constitution. The terms of that constitution require massive corruption to operate, in the absence of a "real" Infallible Imam who actually is infallible. Iran must replace its constitution with one that contains strong checks and balances, or Iran will always be a failed nation, constantly claiming victimhood, blaming it on the West, but always in poverty and chaos.

41.4. Regime change and generational awakening

There is a great desire in the West for something called "regime change" in Iran, although it's rarely specified what that means.

Any of the four scenarios listed above would qualify as a form of "regime change," since it would replace Khamenei. Though whether there would be any real change is questionable.

From the point of view of generational theory, a "regime change" in Iran at the present time would have a specific meaning - an Awakening era climax. The Awakening era is the time, starting around 15 years after the end of a generational crisis war, that the younger generation comes of age and challenges the generations of survivors of the war, creating a "generation gap" or a "generational conflict." The Awakening era climax is a major political event that resolves the generational conflict in favor of the values of the younger generations or the older generations.

An awakening era climax is often called a "Velvet Coup" or "Velvet Revolution," such as the the peaceful 1989 uprising that ousted the Communist regime in the former Czechoslovakia. In America, the 1974 ousting of president Richard Nixon was a climax that firmly established the political victory of the younger post-war generations over the survivors of World War II. It's also possible for it to go in the opposite direction, as the massive 1989 Tiananmen Square massacre firmly established the victory of the Chinese Communist Party over the younger generations.

However, it should not be assumed that Iran will be a better place after the awakening climax. In 1979, if Khomeini's revolution had lost to the Shah, it would have been replaced with a secular government that was just as bad, jailing, torturing and killing just as many people. As I've written before Reza Shaw killed hundreds of Khomeini's followers during the 1963 White Revolution. There were no good guys in 1979. Khomeini was just as bad as the Shah.

Similarly, when the awakening climax occurs, presumably in a victory for the younger generation — the Reformists over the Principlists — it's quite possible, even likely, that the new government would be just as bad, jailing, torturing and killing just as many people as the current government.

One can only hope that when the awakening climax arrives, there will be enough concerned people that they will follow the suggestion of a "constitutional convention," like the one in the US in 1787, where leaders of the Principlists, Moderates and Reformists, along with leaders of the Majlis, the Assembly of Experts, and other commercial, religious and government leaders will be locked in a room, with no communication with the press or the public, and told not to come out until they have a new constitution incorporating the following:

- A constitution which, like the US Constitution, is designed through and through with checks and balances.
- Restoration of the prominence of "popular will" in the Constitution.
- Reduced prominence for "divine guidance," although a formula could be found for including it. A template might be found in the separation of religion and government that prevailed for the millennium following the disappearance of Muhammad Al-Mahdi, the 12th Infallible Imam, in 940 AD.

This is the kind of "regime change" that Iran needs. Selecting a new leader will not be nearly as important as the rules that the new leaders has to obey, as defined by the constitution.

Part X. The End

Chapter 42. About Generational Theory

The easiest way to understand generational theory is to think about American mothers in the 1950s. These mothers are almost universally stereotyped as repressed and controlled, and forced to stay at home, in the kitchen, barefoot and pregnant. This is the stereotype, but absolutely none of it is true.

A 1950s mother would have grown up during the Great Depression, surrounded by homelessness, starvation and bankruptcy. If she herself hadn't been forced to live under a bridge and depend on soup kitchens for food, then she undoubtedly had many friends who had been forced to do so.

Then, as the Great Depression ended, she saw her brothers, father and uncles tortured and maimed on the Bataan Death March, and then shot down like fish in a barrel on the beaches of Normandy. Out of patriotism, she had been forced to take "Rosie the Riveter" type jobs that she hated.

So when the 1950s arrived, a home with a white picket fence where a mother could stay at home with the kids and be safe and dry and warm and reliably supported by a working husband was a gift from heaven. This was a gift that mothers of the 1950s wanted to give to their daughters. They had suffered through starvation, homelessness and slaughter, and they had won, and they wanted to give their daughters the gift of the fruits of that victory.

Unfortunately, their daughters didn't want those gifts. Their scorn and contempt for those gifts gave rise to the women's lib and feminist movements of the 60s and beyond, holding their own mothers and their mothers' values in contempt.

Generational theory is based on the very obvious fact that children rebel against their parents, and so each generation differs significantly from the previous one. These generational changes turn out to be quite predictable, and generational theory captures those predictable changes.

In the 20th century, the foundational work on generational theory was done by several researchers, including Anthony Wallace, William

McLoughlin, Neil Howe and William Strauss. Their research examined generational changes in England and the United States.

In the 21st century, John J. Xenakis has led the development of generational theory on the web site GenerationalDynamics.com. There are thousands of generational analyses and forecasts for hundreds of countries, including Iran, Turkey, China, Pakistan, Sri Lanka, Uganda, and other countries all over the world. These analyses and forecast have proven to be extremely accurate, proving the validity of Generational Dynamics and generational theory. This body of work continues every day, providing a country by country picture of where the world is and where it's going.

Chapter 43. About John J. Xenakis

John J. Xenakis has a varied career. He started out studying mathematics at Massachusetts Institute of Technology, and completed all course and exam requirements for a PhD except the thesis. He spent most of his career as Computer Scientist and Senior Software Engineer, and also wrote thousands of articles as Technology Editor and Analyst for several business and technical publications.

After the attack on New York's World Trade Center on September 11, 2001, Mr. Xenakis became interested in work that had been done earlier on generational theory, and how it seemed to predict that something like the 9/11 attack would occur. He realized generational theory would be useless if it only applied to American and English generations. If generational theory could not be used to analyze and predict current events in all countries at all times, then we would have to assume that the entire theory was based on cherry-picking events in Anglo-American history, and was therefore worthless as a theory, no better than astrology.

He pulled together a number of disciplines — technological forecasting, system dynamics, chaos theory, historical analysis and computational complexity theory — and combined them with generational theory to produce a complete, sophisticated theory called Generational Dynamics, and used the web site GenerationalDynamics.com as a development platform. He's written thousands of analyses and forecasts showing that generational theory is a valid analysis tool for all countries at all times in history.

Mr. Xenakis admits that even he is astonished by how successful Generational Dynamics has been in analyzing and forecasting future events in one country after another. He says, "If you had asked me thirty years ago whether it was even possible to do what I'm doing today, I would have said that it's mathematically impossible." However, in brief, it was the application of Chaos Theory to generational theory that provided the breakthrough, since Chaos Theory tells you exactly what can and cannot be predicted.

The first major test occurred on May 1, 2003, when Xenakis posted an article "Mideast Roadmap - Will it bring peace?" President George Bush had just published his "Mideast Roadmap to Peace" providing specific proposals for a Palestinian state by 2005 side by side with Israel. Xenakis did a detailed generational analysis and showed that the plan would not succeed because Arabs and Jews would be refighting the 1948 war that their great-grandparents' generation had fought, following the United Nations partitioning of Palestine and the creation of the state of Israel.

Xenakis says, "When I posted that analysis, I remember thinking that it might be a completely wrong, that generational theory might be completely wrong. Six months later, the Israelis and Palestinians might have shaken hands on a deal that would create two-states side-by-side, and so forth. My prediction was that it couldn't happen, so if it had happened, then I would have probably have completely dropped my interest in generational theory forever, and gone on to lead a much more normal and probably happier life."

Now, fifteen years and thousands of "World View" analyses and forecasts on hundreds of countries later, this success has been repeated over and over, proving the validity of Generational Dynamics. These analyses can be found on the web site GenerationalDynamics.com

The purpose of this book on Iran is to provide an in-depth Generational Dynamics analysis to the entire span of Persian history, from the early Persian empires to the present time. This book also serves as an additional validation of generational theory by providing a generational analysis of the entire history of a single nation (other than the United States or other Western nations). Books providing similar "World View" analyses of other topics and countries will follow.

Chapter 44. Acknowledgments

I would like to thank author Loretta Napoleoni for her numerous suggestions and for serving as a mentor for bringing this book to market. She is author of the book *ISIS, The Terror Nation*:

https://www.amazon.com/ISIS-Terror-Nation-Loretta-Napoleoni/dp/1609807251

I would like to thank Cynthia Xenakis for proofreading the draft and making valuable suggestions.

I would like to thank Professor Linnea McCord for proofreading the draft and making valuable suggestions. She is author of the book *The Wisdom of Ants: Restore the Secret Power of Trust That Made America Great Before It's Too Late*

https://www.amazon.com/Wisdom-Ants-Restore-Secret-America-ebook/dp/B01GW6JGVE

The picture on the front cover is of Pro-Government demonstrations in Tehran, 2009

The two pictures depicting ancient Persia are from the 1906 book:

Persia Past and Present: A Book Of Travel and Research by A. V. Williams Jackson (Abraham Valentine Williams), 1862-1937

https://archive.org/details/persiapastpresen00jackuoft

Part XI. Footnotes / References

[1] NYT/Reuters(7/11/1999): Student Protests Shake Iran's Government
https://www.nytimes.com/1999/07/11/world/student-protests-shake-iran-s-government.html

[2] NYTimes/Friedman(6/12/2002): Iran / The Best of Enemies?
https://www.nytimes.com/2002/06/12/opinion/the-best-of-enemies.html

[3] NYTimes/ThomasFriedman(6/16/2002): Third generation / Iran's Third Wave
https://www.nytimes.com/2002/06/16/opinion/iran-s-third-wave.html

[4] Britannica: Iranian Revolution of 1978–79
https://www.britannica.com/event/Iranian-Revolution-of-1978-1979

[5] Economist: Iran, 1988 — What happened?
https://www.economist.com/newsbook/2012/06/21/what-happened

[6] Diplomat(7/31/2013): The Forgotten Mass Execution of Prisoners in Iran in 1988
https://thediplomat.com/2013/07/the-forgotten-mass-execution-of-prisoners-in-iran-in-1988/

[7] IranRights-org(4/18/2011,PDF): The Massacre of Political Prisoners in Iran, 1988,
Report Of An Inquiry https://www.iranrights.org/library/document/1380

[8] History-com: Iran Hostage Crisis (11/4/1979 - 1/21/1981)
https://www.history.com/topics/iran-hostage-crisis

[9] Miami-edu: Khomeini's Theory of Islamic State and the Making of the Iranian Revolution - Mehdi Shadmehr
http://moya.bus.miami.edu/~mshadmehr/Ideology.pdf

[10] MideastPolSci(12/21/2017): Roozbeh Safshekan, The Source of Legitimacy in the Guardianship of the Jurist: Historical Genealogy & Political Implications
https://pomeps.org/2017/12/21/the-source-of-legitimacy-in-the-guardianship-of-the-jurist-historical-genealogy-political-implications/

[11] AlIslam-org(Book/PDF)(2010): Guardianship Of The Jurist / A Cursory Glance at the Theory of Wilayat al- Faqih
 https://www.al-islam.org/printpdf/book/export/html/28983

[12] AlIslam-org: What is Wilayat al-Faqih? ; Guardianship of the Jurist
https://www.al-islam.org/shia-political-thought-ahmed-vaezi/what-wilayat-al-faqih

[13] Russiapedia-rt: Of Russian origin: Politburo https://russiapedia.rt.com/of-russian-origin/politburo/

[14] Brookings(2/9/2016): Everything you need to know about Iran's Assembly of Experts election
https://www.brookings.edu/blog/markaz/2016/02/09/everything-you-need-to-know-about-irans-assembly-of-experts-election/

[15] IranicaOnline(2/23/2012): Guardian Council
http://www.iranicaonline.org/articles/guardian-council

[16] MEQuarterly(2009): Sword verses / Are Judaism and Christianity as Violent as Islam? http://www.meforum.org/2159/are-judaism-and-christianity-as-violent-as-islam

[17] Britannica: Jizya / Jizyah https://www.britannica.com/topic/jizya

[18] ReformJudaism(Spring,2013): Holy War in Judaism: The Fall and Rise of a Controversial Idea https://reformjudaism.org/jewish-life/arts-culture/literature/holy-war-judaism-fall-and-rise-controversial-idea

[19] LastProphet-info: Tabouk / 630 / Byzantines 36 - The Tabuk Campaign Dr Casim Avci http://www.lastprophet.info/36-the-tabuk-campaign

[20] BBC: Salman Rushdie and 'Satanic Verses' / 1989: Ayatollah sentences author to death
http://news.bbc.co.uk/onthisday/hi/dates/stories/february/14/newsid_2541000/2541149.stm

[21] IndiaTimes(2/24/2016): Iran imposes new $600,000 fatwa on author Salman Rushdie https://economictimes.indiatimes.com/magazines/panache/iran-imposes-new-600000-fatwa-on-author-salman-rushdie/articleshow/51124985.cms

[22] BBC(1/14/2015): Charlie Hebdo attack: Three days of terror (1/7-9/2015) https://www.bbc.com/news/world-europe-30708237

[23] MichaelNugent(5/5/2009): History of Irish blasphemy law https://www.michaelnugent.com/2009/05/05/history-of-irish-blasphemy-law/

[24] ExpressTribune-pk/AFP(5/5/2011): Pakistan / The history of the blasphemy law https://tribune.com.pk/story/99414/the-history-of-the-blasphemy-law/

[25] NewAdvent: Persia http://www.newadvent.org/cathen/11712a.htm

[26] Britannica: Zoroaster / Zarathustra https://www.britannica.com/biography/Zarathustra

[27] CrystalLinks: Arsacid Empire / Parthian Empire 247 BC - 224 AD http://www.crystalinks.com/Parthian_Empire.html

[28] ClassicalWisdom(PDF): The Roman-Parthian Wars By Cam Rea https://classicalwisdom.com/wp-content/uploads/2015/ebooks/romeparthia.pdf

[29] JewishVirtualLibrary: Philosophical dualism / Moral dualism / Zoroastrianism / Dualism http://www.jewishvirtuallibrary.org/dualism

[30] Guardian(10/4/2006): Zoroastrianism / Ancient religions clash in modern Iran https://www.theguardian.com/world/2006/oct/04/worlddispatch.iran

[31] JoshuaProject: 1893 massacre / Hazaras - Introduction / History https://joshuaproject.net/people_groups/12076/AF

[32] IranChamber: History of Iran - Qajar Dynasty http://www.iranchamber.com/history/qajar/qajar.php

[33] HomaKatouzian-com(9/2011): The Revolution for Law: A Chronographic Analysis of the Constitutional Revolution of Iran http://homakatouzian.com/?p=617

[34] ConstitutionProject: Iran (Islamic Republic of)'s Constitution of 1979 with Amendments through 1989
https://www.constituteproject.org/constitution/Iran_1989.pdf?lang=en

[35] Cambridge-org(PDF): Firoozeh Kashani-Sabet - Fragile Frontiers: The Diminishing Domains Of Qajar Iran https://www.cambridge.org/core/services/aop-cambridge-core/content/view/DF7E804F3038E9C8D4174DA32501E83C/S0020743800064473a.pdf/fragile_frontiers_the_diminishing_domains_of_qajar_iran.pdf

[36] MetropolitanMuseum(2004): The Achaemenid Persian Empire (550–330 B.C.) https://www.metmuseum.org/toah/hd/acha/hd_acha.htm

[37] BahaiStories(4/1/2012): Mirza Buzurg / Bahai / Baha'u'llah's Childhood and Youth http://bahaistories.blogspot.com/2012/04/bahaullahs-childhood-and-youth.html

[38] Poets-org: The Charge of the Light Brigade - Alfred Lord Tennyson, 1809 - 1892 https://www.poets.org/poetsorg/poem/charge-light-brigade

[39] EncyclopediaIranica: Anglo-Persian War (1856-57)
http://www.iranicaonline.org/articles/anglo-persian-war-1856-57

[40] EncyclopediaIranica: Concessions / Russia / Britain / Tobacco revolt
http://www.iranicaonline.org/articles/concessions

[41] WhatWhenHow: Ottoman / Capitulations, Middle East (Western Colonialism)
http://what-when-how.com/western-colonialism/capitulations-middle-east-western-colonialism/

[42] VirginiaTech: Chapter 8 The Tobacco Movement (1890-92)
https://vtechworks.lib.vt.edu/bitstream/handle/10919/30008/CHAPTER_VIII_TOBACCO.pdf?sequence=20

[43] NYU: A Brief History of 20th-Century Iran
https://greyartgallery.nyu.edu/2015/12/a-brief-history-of-20th-century-iran/

[44] IranReview(6/20/2016): June-23-1908 / The Bombardemant of Iran's Majlis: After 108 Years
http://www.iranreview.org/content/Documents/Contemporary_History_The_Bombardemant_of_Majlis_June_23rd_1908.htm

[45] IranReview(8/4/2016): Iran and the First World War
http://www.iranreview.org/content/Documents/Iran-and-the-First-World-War.htm

[46] IranChamber: History of Iran - Pahlavi Dynasty
http://www.iranchamber.com/history/pahlavi/pahlavi.php

[47] IranChamber: History of Iran - Mohammad Reza Shah Pahlavi
http://www.iranchamber.com/history/mohammad_rezashah/mohammad_rezashah.php

[48] State.gov(6/15/2017): Foreign Relations of the United States, 1952-1954, Iran, 1951–1954 https://history.state.gov/historicaldocuments/frus1951-54Iran/pressrelease

[49] SanJoseStateUniv: Mohammad Mossadeq, the Nationalization of the Anglo-Iranian Oil Company and the Attempted Overthrow of the Shah
http://www.sjsu.edu/faculty/watkins/mossadeq.htm

[50] EncyclopediaIranica: Anglo-Persian Oil Company
http://www.iranicaonline.org/articles/anglo-persian-oil-company

[51] EncyclopediaIranica: IRAN ii. IRANIAN HISTORY (1) Pre-Islamic Times
http://www.iranicaonline.org/articles/iran-ii1-pre-islamic-times

[52] Investopedia: Minsky Moment
https://www.investopedia.com/terms/m/minskymoment.asp

[53] Jrank-org: Spengler / Toynbee / Braudel / Cycles - The Twentieth Century
http://science.jrank.org/pages/8918/Cycles-Twentieth-Century.html

[54] JewishVirtualLibrary: Elam http://www.jewishvirtuallibrary.org/elam

[55] TimesOfIsrael(3/8/2018): Who is King Cyrus, and why did Netanyahu compare him to Trump? https://www.timesofisrael.com/who-is-king-cyrus-and-why-is-netanyahu-comparing-him-to-trump/

[56] AncientHistory-eu(5/29/2012): Seleucus / Seleucid Empire / Seleucus I Nicator (358-281 BC) https://www.ancient.eu/Seleucos_I/

[57] Bond-edu-au(12/1/2005): Rome and Parthia: Power politics and diplomacy across cultural frontiers
https://epublications.bond.edu.au/cgi/viewcontent.cgi?article=1009&context=cewces_papers

[58] AncientHistory-eu: Parsa / Persepolis https://www.ancient.eu/persepolis/

[59] BBC(7/15/2012): Podcasts / Alexander the not so Great: History through Persian eyes https://www.bbc.com/news/magazine-18803290

[60] AncientHistory-eu: Sassanian Empire 226-651 AD
http://www.ancient.eu/Sasanian_Empire/

[61] VictoriaAzad-ParvanehPourshariati(2008,PDF): Decline and Fall of the Sasanian Empire
http://www.victoriaazad.com/pdf/Decline_and_Fall_of_the_Sasanian_Empire.pdf

[62] Wikishia: Descriptions of 12 imams / summary table / Imams of the Shi'a
http://en.wikishia.net/view/Imams_of_the_Shi%27a

[63] Al-Islam.org: History of The Caliphs From the Death of the Messenger (S), to the Decline of the 'Umayyad Dynasty 11-132 AH [[132->750-AD]] https://www.al-islam.org/history-of-the-caliphs-rasul-jafariyan

[64] Al-Islam-org: First Shia Imam / 601-661 / Ali ibn Abi Talib, the Fourth Caliph of the Muslims https://www.al-islam.org/restatement-history-islam-and-muslims-sayyid-ali-ashgar-razwy/ali-ibn-abi-talib-fourth-caliph

[65] Britannica: Islamic World / Conversion and crystallization (634–870)
https://www.britannica.com/topic/Islamic-world/Conversion-and-crystallization-634-870

[66] Fikreraza(book,pdf): Manifestations Of The Moon Of Prophethood
http://www.fikreraza.org/books/books/manifestations-of-the-moon-of-prophethood%5B1%5D.pdf

[67] Archive-org: Qadisiyya / Book: Battle of Al- Qadisiyya, The Fall of the Mighty Persian Empire - Abdul Malik Mujahid https://archive.org/details/the-battle-of-qadisiyyah-the-fall-of-the-mighty-persian-empire.pdf

[68] Iranica: Battle of Qadisiyya http://www.iranicaonline.org/articles/qadesiya-battle

[69] DiscoveringIslam: Jew: Abdullah ibn Saba / Origins of the Shia Sect
http://www.discoveringislam.org/origins_of_shiism.htm

[70] Mohammed marries 9 yo Aisha / "Why are You Agitated by the Age of 'Aisha?"-Dr Jonathan Brown https://www.lamppostproductions.com/dr-johnathon-brown-on-the-age-of-aisha/

[71] UnderstandingKoran: A Short Biography of Aisha, the Mother of the Believers [Learn Tajweed with UQA] http://understandquran.com/short-biography-aisha-mother-believers-learn-tajweed-uqa.html

[72] Girlshealth-gov: Girl's puberty / Timing and stages of puberty
https://www.girlshealth.gov/body/puberty/timing.html

[73] InnocenceProject: DNA Exonerations in the United States
https://www.innocenceproject.org/dna-exonerations-in-the-united-states/

[74] Al-Islam.org: Battle of Karbala, the Chain of Events https://www.al-islam.org/articles/karbala-the-chain-of-events-ramzan-sabir

[75] Britannica: Battle of Karbala https://www.britannica.com/event/Battle-of-Karbala

[76] DailyMail(10/12/2016): Ashura - Descriptions and photos of flagellation and blood-letting around the world http://www.dailymail.co.uk/news/article-3834183/A-little-girl-Chennai-India-prepares-scalp-slashed-open-children-smear-BLOOD-Islamic-ceremony-mourning-death-Prophet-s-grandson.html

[77] GlobalSecurity(5/7/2011): Fivers / Houthis / Yemen / Zaydi Islam
https://www.globalsecurity.org/military/intro/islam-zaydi.htm

[78] Dawn(11/26/2012): Hussaini Brahmins Brahmans / Karbala and how Lahore was involved https://www.dawn.com/news/766877

[79] TimesIndia(11/5/2014): Brahmins / For Hussaini brahmans, it's Muharram as usual https://timesofindia.indiatimes.com/city/delhi/For-Hussaini-brahmans-its-Muharram-as-usual/articleshow/45039950.cms

[80] RealmOfHistory(11/16/2015): Banquet of Blood: Abbasids wipe out their opponents in a single night of feasting and gore

https://www.realmofhistory.com/2015/11/16/banquet-of-blood-abbasids-wipe-out-their-opponents-in-a-single-night-of-feasting-and-gore/

[81] Britannica: Abbasid dynasty https://www.britannica.com/topic/Abbasid-dynasty

[82] DavidDerrick-ToynbeeConvector(7/15/2007): Stony ground: Roman law and Sharia https://davidderrick.wordpress.com/2007/07/15/stony-ground-roman-law-and-sharia/

[83] McGill-ca(8/2004): Ayman Daher - The Sharia: Roman Law Wearing An Islamic Veil? https://www.mcgill.ca/classics/files/classics/2004-08.pdf

[84] Wikipedia: Islam Comparison chart: Sunni, Shia, Ibadi Islam https://en.wikipedia.org/wiki/Differences_between_Sunni,_Shia_and_Ibadi_Islam

[85] BibleOdyssey/BrendanBreed: What Are the Earliest Versions and Translations of the Bible? https://www.bibleodyssey.org/en/tools/bible-basics/what-are-the-earliest-versions-and-translations-of-the-bible

[86] ChristianityToday: Athanasius / Decided the 27 books of the New Testament - 367 AD https://www.christianitytoday.com/history/people/theologians/athanasius.html

[87] CUNY-Pecorino-1: Pecorino - online textbook - Origins of the Koran http://www.qcc.cuny.edu/SocialSciences/ppecorino/INTRO_TEXT/Chapter%203%20Religion/Koran-Origins.htm

[88] IslamicWeb: Mohammed's secretary / collected Koran / Zayd ibn Thabit http://islamicweb.com/history/sahaba/bio.ZAYD_IBN_THABIT.htm

[89] ExploringIslam: Sunnah vs. Hadith http://www.exploring-islam.com/difference-between-sunnah-and-hadith.html

[90] ISunnah-com: List of Sunnah http://www.isunnah.com/sunnah_list.html

[91] Sunnah-com: Exhaustive list of Hadith https://www.sunnah.com/

[92] FaithFreedom/IbnKammuna(3/10/2013): Koran / December 632 AD / The Yamama battle and the preservation of the Qur'an http://www.faithfreedom.org/the-yamama-battle-and-the-preservation-of-the-quran/

[93] Stortinget-no: Norway / The Constitution https://www.stortinget.no/en/In-English/About-the-Storting/The-Constitution/

[94] Wipo-int: Belgium - The Belgian Constitution http://www.wipo.int/wipolex/en/details.jsp?id=11637

[95] Napoleon-org: Was Napoleonic France a "state based on law"? https://www.napoleon.org/en/history-of-the-two-empires/articles/napoleonic-france-state-based-law/

[96] History.com: Separation of Powers / Checks and Balances / FDR packs Supreme Court https://www.history.com/topics/checks-and-balances

[97] Anadolu(5/3/2018): OPINION - Four scenarios for post-Khamenei Iran https://www.aa.com.tr/en/analysis-news/opinion-four-scenarios-for-post-khamenei-iran/1080283

[98] RadioFarda(2/24/2018): Transparency International Ranks Iran Among Most Corrupt Countries https://en.radiofarda.com/a/iran-ranks-low-on-transparency-index-2017/29060266.html

[99] Aawsat(4/3/2018): Gholam Ali Jafarzadeh Emenabadi / Iranian Deputy Calls for Fighting Corruption in Khamenei Office https://aawsat.com/english/home/article/1225696/iranian-deputy-calls-fighting-corruption-khamenei-office

[100] GanAntiCorruptionPortal(4/2017): Iran Corruption Report
https://www.business-anti-corruption.com/country-profiles/iran/

[101] AlJaz(1/3/2018): Why did protests erupt in Iran?
https://www.aljazeera.com/indepth/opinion/protests-erupt-iran-180101142214891.html

[102] AP(1/3/2018): 2009 vs. 2018: How Iran's new protests compare to the 'Green Movement' of the past
https://www.thestar.com/news/world/2018/01/03/2009-vs-2018-how-irans-new-protests-compare-to-the-green-movement-of-the-past.html

[103] GenerationalDynamics: 9-Sep-16 World View — Saudi Arabia makes a dangerous accusation - that Iranians are 'not Muslims'
http://www.generationaldynamics.com/pg/xct.gd.e160909.htm#e160909

[104] GenerationalDynamics: 25-May-16 World View — Iran-India sign 'historic' Chabahar port deal to counter Pakistan-China
http://www.generationaldynamics.com/pg/xct.gd.e160525.htm#e160525

[105] GenerationalDynamics: 29-Dec-14 World View — Do news organizations ignore jihadist attacks on Christians?
http://www.generationaldynamics.com/pg/xct.gd.e141229.htm#e141229

[106] GenerationalDynamics: 18-Apr-11 News — Russia's Muslims vs Christians on the National Emblem and on polygamy
http://www.generationaldynamics.com/pg/xct.gd.e110418b.htm#e110418b

[107] GenerationalDynamics: 30-Dec-17 World View — Anti-government, anti-war and economic protests spread across Iran
http://www.generationaldynamics.com/pg/xct.gd.e171230.htm#e171230

[108] Generational Dynamics: 10-Jan-15 World View — Up to 2000 Nigeria civilians killed in three-day Boko Haram massacre
http://www.generationaldynamics.com/pg/xct.gd.e150110.htm#e150110

Made in the USA
Middletown, DE
27 September 2018